# Alliances™ Revealed

## A Review of the Alliances™ Edition of Magic: The Gathering®

## by George H. Baxter

## Wordware Publishing, Inc.

**Library of Congress Cataloging-in-Publication Data**

Baxter, George H.
    Alliances revealed : a review of the Alliances edition of Magic:
    the Gathering / George H. Baxter.
        p.    cm.
    Includes index.
    ISBN 1-55622-521-0 (pbk.)
    1. Magic: The Gathering (Game)    2. Playing cards.    I. Title.
    GV1469.62.M34B39     1996
    793.93'2—dc20                     96-34122
                                            CIP

Copyright © 1997, George H. Baxter

Interior book illustrations © Christopher Pickrell, Heath, Ohio

All Rights Reserved

No part of this book may be reproduced in any form or by any means
without permission in writing from Wordware Publishing, Inc.

Printed in the United States of America

ISBN 1-55622-521-0

10 9 8 7 6 5 4 3 2 1

9607

The Duelist, Ice Age, Alliances, and Deckmaster are trademarks and Magic: The Gathering and
Wizards of the Coast are registered trademarks of Wizards of the Coast, Inc.

This book is not affiliated with or sponsored by Wizards of the Coast, Inc.

All inquiries for volume purchases of this book should be addressed to Wordware
Publishing, Inc., at 1506 Capital Avenue, Plano, Texas 75074. Telephone inquiries
may be made by calling:

(214) 423-0090

# Contents

Many thanks to Regan Reece for his aid in editing this work.

This book is dedicated to my Mom and Dad.

# Introduction

*Alliances Revealed* takes an in-depth look at the cards added in the new set, Alliances. The Alliances set is one of the strongest additions to the Magic Card pool since Antiquities. Besides a number of new tournament-level cards, the Alliances set also adds a whole new concept to Magic with its pitch cards (cards that can be cast by discarding an extra card instead of paying their casting cost).

This book was written for the advanced player, and to get the most out of it a good understanding of deck construction is essential.

*Alliances Revealed* also details sixteen tournament-level decks, including the top decks from the 1996 Nationals. Each of the decks contains Alliances cards and each one is of the highest level of quality.

| | |
|---|---|
| **Card Name:** | *Ashnod's Cylix* |
| **Casting Cost:** | 2 |
| **Card Type:** | Artifact |
| **Card Text:** | 3, T: Target player looks at the top three cards of his or her library and puts one of them on top of that library. Remove the remaining two from the game. |

**Ashnod's Cylix Revealed:** The true potential of this card lies in its combination with Sylvan Library. This gives a player the ability to view up to three new cards a turn. A player can take the one card out of the group of three that he wants, then use the Cylix to remove the remaining two. This card can also serve as a makeshift Millstone. The fact that the cards it eliminates are removed from the game makes its effect harder to counter than the Millstones (e.g., Feldon's Cane). One could use it as yet another means for destroying an opponent's library.

| | |
|---|---|
| **Card Name:** | *Astrolabe* |
| **Casting Cost:** | 3 |
| **Card Type:** | Artifact |
| **Card Text:** | 1, T: Sacrifice Astrolabe to add two mana of any color to your mana pool. Play this ability as an interrupt. Draw a card at the beginning of the next turn's upkeep. |

**Astrolabe Revealed:** The Astrolabe is yet another cantrip. It is my opinion that this is one of the weaker cards in the set. Its casting cost makes it difficult to use effectively. This card may be useful in multicolor decks that use a variety of cards with two of a specific color in their casting cost.

| | |
|---|---|
| **Card Name:** | *Floodwater Dam* |
| **Casting Cost:** | 3 |
| **Card Type:** | Artifact |
| **Card Text:** | XX1, T: Tap X target lands. |

**Floodwater Dam Revealed:** Floodwater Dam is one of the cards in the Alliances set that could provide a new lock combination. This card can be extremely powerful if used with a Mana Flare, effectively locking down an opponent's land during his upkeep and rendering him helpless. Independently it is too expensive to activate. To tap only two of an opponent's land it would cost its caster five mana, making it very difficult to use without any mana enhancement.

| | |
|---|---|
| **Card Name:** | *Gustha's Scepter* |
| **Casting Cost:** | 0 |
| **Card Type:** | Artifact |
| **Card Text:** | If Gustha's Scepter leaves play or you lose control of it, put all cards under Gustha's Scepter into your graveyard. |

T: Put any card from your hand face down under Gustha's Scepter. You may look at that card at any time. T: Return any card under Gustha's Scepter to your hand.

**Gustha's Scepter Revealed:** Gustha's Scepter allows its controller to moderate his hand size and protect cards from hand destruction. A player can save one card from a Hymn to Tourach with the Scepter, safely tucking it away until needed. This card is more powerful in Type I than in Type II. For example, when used with a Time Twister or Wheel of Fortune it can save cards from being discarded or reshuffled into the deck.

| | |
|---|---|
| **Card Name:** | *Helm of Obedience* |
| **Casting Cost:** | 4 |
| **Card Type:** | Artifact |
| **Card Text:** | X and tap: Put the top card of target opponent's library into his or her graveyard. Continue doing this until you have put X cards or a creature card into the graveyard, whichever occurs first. If the last card put into the graveyard is a creature card, bury Helm of Obedience and put that creature into play under your control as though it were just cast. X cannot be equal to 0. |

**Helm of Obedience Revealed:** The Helm is one of the strongest cards in the Alliances set. This card will more than likely terminate the creatureless decks. The Helm's power is obvious, and it in combination with Millstones will speed deck destruction and make a more common and viable road to victory. It is easy to quickly overestimate the Helm though. The most powerful aspect of the Helm is its ability to remove cards, not its ability to control creatures. It is not comparable to a Control Magic because the creature gained is not drawn or cast by the opponent and thus provides no card count economy. Also, the creature is not selected. For example, a player might use the Helm to draw a Nightmare when he has no swamps, or to draw a Llanowar Elves. This card will frequent more sideboards than regular decks, existing as the bane of all creatureless decks in Magic.

| | |
|---|---|
| **Card Name:** | *Lodestone Bauble* |
| **Casting Cost:** | 0 |
| **Card Type:** | Artifact |
| **Card Text:** | 1, T: Sacrifice Lodestone Bauble to put up to four target basic lands from any player's graveyard on top of his or her library in any order. That player draws a card at the beginning of the next turn's upkeep. |

**Lodestone Bauble Revealed:** The Lodestone Bauble will greatly affect the power of one-shot land destruction decks as well as the popular Erhnamgeddon and Jokulhaups decks, which will probably include the Bauble. A player could ensure a speedy recovery from an Armageddon or Jokulhaups by using the Bauble. Its entrance to the Magic environment will limit land destruction but will far from overwhelm it. The Lodestone's controller will still only lay one land a turn, providing the LB player a speed advantage.

| Card Name: | *Mishra's Groundbreaker* |
|---|---|
| Casting Cost: | 4 |
| Card Type: | Artifact |
| Card Text: | Tap: Sacrifice Mishra's Groundbreaker. Target land becomes a 3/3 artifact creature. That creature still counts as a land. |

**Mishra's Groundbreaker Revealed:** The Groundbreaker is not a particularly strong card: its expense overshadows its ability. The first and obvious expense is its high casting cost. Its user pays the same casting cost as an Erhnam and receives a 3/3 creature instead of a 4/5 creature. Its other major cost is that of a card, the Groundbreaker itself. This card might work with Balance or Wrath of God. After casting either one of these cards you can instantly have the first new creature in play.

| Card Name: | *Mystic Compass* |
|---|---|
| Casting Cost: | 2 |
| Card Type: | Artifact |
| Card Text: | 1, T: Target mana-producing land becomes a basic land type of your choice until end of turn. |

**Mystic Compass Revealed:** A first impression of the Mystic Compass may classify the card as a cheaper version of the Celestial Prism. However, the Compass is actually more versatile because a player can use it on an opponent's land as well as his own. This could prove useful during the upkeep, denying an opponent a specific color of mana from one of his lands in play. It might also assist landwalking creatures by turning an opponent's land into the type required for the landwalking ability.

| | |
|---|---|
| **Card Name:** | *Phyrexian Portal* |
| **Casting Cost:** | 3 |
| **Card Type:** | Artifact |
| **Card Text:** | 3: Target opponent looks at the top ten cards of your library and separates them into two face-down piles. Choose one of those piles and remove it from the game. Search the remaining pile and put one of those cards into your hand. Shuffle the remaining cards into your library. Ignore this effect if you have fewer than ten cards in your library. |

**Phyrexian Portal Revealed:** This card is very strong, but it definitely has its drawbacks. It works not only as a cheap Jayemdae Tome, but also as a pseudo-Demonic Tutor. It is only useable about six to nine times a game in a regular 60-card deck, but if used only twice it almost pays for itself. The Portal also adds a psychological element to the game, allowing an opponent to make two different stacks and forcing the controller to choose one of the two.

| | |
|---|---|
| **Card Name:** | *Scarab of the Unseen* |
| **Casting Cost:** | 2 |
| **Card Type:** | Artifact |
| **Card Text:** | T: Sacrifice Scarab of the Unseen to return all enchantments on target permanent you own to their owners' hand. Draw a card at the beginning of the next turn's upkeep. |

**Scarab of the Unseen Revealed:** The Scarab of the Unseen is one of several cards in the Alliances set that seems to reward the use of creature enchantments. This card helps reduce the card advantage an opponent gains when he removes an enchanted creature (e.g., casting a Lightning Bolt on a Black Knight with an Unholy Strength). Since the card is a cantrip it makes it much easier to place it into a deck. An interesting combination is to use the Scarab with Bestial Fury. The controller pulls an extra card after recasting the Bestial Fury, because both the Scarab and the Fury are cantrips. This means when the Fury is recast the controller nets one extra card. Nevertheless it is still worthless.

| | |
|---|---|
| **Card Name:** | *Sol Grail* |
| **Casting Cost:** | 3 |
| **Card Type:** | Artifact |
| **Card Text:** | When Sol Grail comes into play, choose a color. T: Add one mana of the chosen color to your mana pool. Play this ability as an interrupt. |

**Sol Grail Revealed:** The Sol Grail is yet another source of artifact mana. This card is not one I expect to see used widely in tournament level decks. Its expense outweighs its benefits.

| | |
|---|---|
| **Card Name:** | *Soldevi Digger* |
| **Casting Cost:** | 2 |
| **Card Type:** | Artifact |
| **Card Text:** | 2: Put the top card of your graveyard on the bottom of your library. |

**Soldevi Digger Revealed:** The Digger is one of the gems in the Alliances set. In combination with any card that allows you to shuffle your deck, the Digger allows a player the opportunity to recycle cards, increasing the frequency of those cards in the game. For instance, if you face an artifact heavy deck, you may use the Digger to constantly add artifact breakers from the graveyard back to the deck. In Type I this card transcends "good" and becomes "ridiculous." There is the obvious use: using the Digger to recycle the power cards (Time Walk, Ancestral Recall, etc.). But the Digger also provides the possibility of an infinite turn combo. You can achieve this with Demonic Consultation and Time Walk: a player casts the Time Walk, uses the Digger to place it on the bottom of the deck, consults for the Time Walk, recasts the Time Walk, and once again uses the Digger to place it on the bottom of the deck.

| Card Name: | ***Storm Cauldron*** |
|---|---|
| **Casting Cost:** | 5 |
| **Card Type:** | Artifact |
| **Card Text:** | During each player's turn, that player may put one additional land into play. Whenever a land is tapped for mana, return that land to owner's hand. |

**Storm Cauldron Revealed:** Like the Soldevi Digger, the Storm Cauldron is another ridiculously strong card. Used with Stasis, a player can achieve an infinite Stasis lock with relative ease, perpetuating the Stasis with only one island. Once a player taps the island to pay for the Stasis's upkeep, it returns to his hand. Though the Stasis is less effective against an opponent's land, it will still lock down any other permanents. Like the Digger, this card is much more threatening in Type I than in Type II. A player could use it in conjunction with Black Vises and force an opponent to take damage for each of the lands returned to his hand.

| Card Name: | ***Whirling Catapult*** |
|---|---|
| **Casting Cost:** | 4 |
| **Card Type:** | Artifact |
| **Card Text:** | 2: Remove the top two cards of your library from the game to have Whirling Catapult deal 1 damage to each creature with flying and each player. |

**Whirling Catapult Revealed:** This card is garbage. Do not expect it in many tournament-level decks. Its casting cost and activation costs are simply too high for its effect, although in sealed deck or booster draft this card could be very useful. Its ability to kill flyers could provide its controller the edge necessary to stop the popular weenie flight decks.

# Artifact Creatures

| | |
|---|---|
| **Card Name:** | *Aesthir Glider* |
| **Casting Cost:** | 3 |
| **Card Type:** | Artifact Creature (2/1) |
| **Card Text:** | Flying. Cannot be assigned to block. |

**Aesthir Glider Revealed:** The Aesthir Glider is very expensive for a 2/1 flyer that cannot block. There are a few uses for it though. In an Abyss deck the Glider could prove useful. There are very few flying artifact creatures to block it once an Abyss is in play. The Glider may also prove strong in sealed deck and booster draft, providing an invaluable flyer that could be employed regardless of the colors you commit to.

| | |
|---|---|
| **Card Name:** | *Phyrexian Devourer* |
| **Casting Cost:** | 6 |
| **Card Type:** | Artifact Creature (1/1) |
| **Card Text:** | If Phyrexian Devourer's power is 7 or greater, bury it. 0: Remove the top card of your library from the game to put a |

+X/+X counter on Phyrexian Devourer, where X is equal to that card's casting cost.

**Phyrexian Devourer Revealed:** This is yet another artifact creature that is not really worth its cost. At best the Devourer can be a 6/6 creature for the cost of six mana. It could be interesting if used in conjunction with a Sylvan Library. A player could place less useful cards on the top of his graveyard to increase the Devourer's power, while cycling through his deck at the same time. This combination is limited, of course, by the size of the Devourer. In order to continue the cycling effect, a player might use cards like Unstable Mutation, enabling the player to remove counters. But then, a player might also choose to smoke crack.

| | |
|---|---|
| **Card Name:** | *Phyrexian War Beast* |
| **Casting Cost:** | 3 |
| **Card Type:** | Artifact Creature (3/4) |
| **Card Text:** | If Phyrexian War Beast leaves play, sacrifice a land, and Phyrexian War Beast deals 1 damage to you. |

**Phyrexian War Beast Revealed:** The War Beast is the strongest of the Alliances artifact creatures. Though the cost of its leaving play is high, its cheap casting cost and high power and toughness make it ideal for a fast creature deck. Consider that this creature can come out on the first turn with Dark Ritual, it is strong enough to sustain a Lightning Bolt, and it seems almost worth utilizing. Almost.

| | |
|---|---|
| **Card Name:** | *Shield Sphere* |
| **Casting Cost:** | 0 |
| **Card Type:** | Artifact Creature (0/6) |
| **Card Text:** | Counts as a wall. If Shield Sphere is assigned as a blocker, put a -0/-1 counter on it. |

**Shield Sphere Revealed:** The Shield Sphere is a nice supplement to decks that need time to develop. For example, if an opponent played a Savannah Lion on the first turn, and you needed four turns to lay enough land to cast a Serrated Arrows to remove it, the Shield Sphere could provide that time.

| | |
|---|---|
| **Card Name:** | *Soldevi Sentry* |
| **Casting Cost:** | 1 |
| **Card Type:** | Artifact Creature (1/1) |
| **Card Text:** | 1: Regenerate. Target opponent may draw a card. |

**Soldevi Sentry Revealed:** Any 1/1 creature for one mana with a special ability is worth its cost and useful for fortifying any number of decks. The disadvantage of its special ability can become an advantage in a deck that employs both Millstones and Howling Mines. Next to the Phyrexian War Beast, the Soldevi Sentry is perhaps the best artifact creature in the Alliances set.

**13**

| | |
|---|---|
| **Card Name:** | *Soldevi Steam Beast* |
| **Casting Cost:** | 5 |
| **Card Type:** | Artifact Creature (4/2) |
| **Card Text:** | Whenever Soldevi Steam Beast becomes tapped, target opponent gains 2 life. 2: Regenerate. |

**Soldevi Steam Beast Revealed:** The Soldevi Steam Beast is one of the stranger creatures in the Alliances set. Its high casting cost and awkward ability recommend a Clay Statue will work better. When the Beast attacks it must tap, meaning that the opponent will only take two damage if the Beast is unblocked. Each time the Beast regenerates, it must tap and the opponent gains two life.

| | |
|---|---|
| **Card Name:** | *Urza's Engine* |
| **Casting Cost:** | 5 |
| **Card Type:** | Artifact Creature (1/5) |
| **Card Text:** | Trample. 3: Banding until end of turn. 3: All creatures banded with Urza's Engine gain trample until end of turn. |

**Urza's Engine Revealed:** Urza's Engine is Bloomingdale's-expensive garbage for morons. The Engine is more of a multiplayer card than a worthwhile tournament level card. Because the creature's special ability has such a high activation cost, it's ineffective and silly.

# Lands

| | |
|---|---|
| **Card Name:** | *Balduvian Trading Post* |
| **Card Type:** | Land |
| **Card Text:** | When Balduvian Trading Post comes into play, sacrifice an untapped mountain or bury Balduvian Trading Post. T: Add 1R to your mana pool. 1, T: Balduvian Trading Post deals 1 damage to target attacking creature. |

**Balduvian Trading Post Revealed:** The Balduvian Trading Post aids any deck with Lightning Bolts. With the Trading Post in play, a red player can use the Post in conjunction with a Lightning Bolt to eliminate an attacking Serra Angel or Vampire. This land, like many, special-assists any Disk deck with red. The Trading Post's major disadvantage is that if removed, an opponent enjoys a two-for-one card advantage. Remember also that the Trading Post can be tapped for mana when it comes into play whether or not its controller sacrifices an untapped mountain. This enables the Trading Post an alternative use as a miniature Dark Ritual for red.

| | |
|---|---|
| **Card Name:** | *Heart of Yavimaya* |
| **Card Type:** | Land |
| **Card Text:** | When Heart of Yavimaya comes into play, sacrifice a forest or bury Heart of Yavimaya. T: Add G to your mana pool. T: Target creature gets +1/+1 until end of turn. |

**Heart of Yavimaya Revealed:** The Heart of Yavimaya is the weakest of the colored special lands in the Alliances set. Its ability to give a creature +1/+1 is not really a justification for the sacrifice of a forest. Though I might use this card in an all-green deck or a sealed or draft environment, I would not put it into many tournament-level constructed decks.

| | |
|---|---|
| **Card Name:** | *Kjeldoran Outpost* |
| **Card Type:** | Land |
| **Card Text:** | When Kjeldoran Outpost comes into play, sacrifice a plains or bury Kjeldoran Outpost. T: Add W to your mana pool. 1W, T: Put a soldier token into play. Treat this token as a 1/1 white creature. |

**Kjeldoran Outpost Revealed:** The Kjeldoran Outpost towers above the other colored special lands in the Alliances set. Its ability to create masses of Soldiers that cannot be countered is awesome. In Ice Age/Alliances formats, this card sits near the top of the heap. The Kjeldoran Outpost is also a must for any white weenie deck. In the late game, most white weenie decks have little or no use for excess land, and the sacrifice of one land for a white creature generator is no sacrifice at all.

| Card Name: | *Lake of the Dead* |
|---|---|
| Card Type: | Land |
| Card Text: | When Lake of the Dead comes into play, sacrifice a swamp or bury Lake of the Dead. T: Add B to your mana pool. T: Sacrifice a swamp to add BBBB to your mana pool. |

**Lake of the Dead Revealed:** The Lake of the Dead is yet another card that makes the all-black deck more deadly than before. Any black player with Lake of the Dead can now use the ability to conjure monstrous Drain Lifes and Sol Burns. In a black deck I would probably not use more than one Lake of the Dead. Sacrificing land can severely drain any deck's resources.

| Card Name: | *School of the Unseen* |
|---|---|
| Card Type: | Land |
| Card Text: | T: Add one colorless mana to your mana pool. 2, T: Add one mana of any color to your mana pool. |

**School of the Unseen Revealed:** The School of the Unseen really does not fit into many decks. Its ability to provide a mana of any color for two colorless is more expensive than it appears. When you activate the School you tap three lands. In most cases, a City of Brass accomplishes the task more readily.

**Card Name:**   *Sheltered Valley*

**Card Type:**   Land

**Card Text:**   When Sheltered Valley comes into play, bury any other Sheltered Valley you control. During your upkeep, if you control three or fewer lands, gain 1 life. T: Add one colorless mana to your mana pool.

**Sheltered Valley Revealed:** The Sheltered Valley assists decks that require very little mana to operate. One can use it in conjunction with Stormbind or Land's Edge. Another use would be in a deck that has a large number of low casting cost spells like Lightning Bolts, Elves, and Archers. Many may scoff at the Sheltered Valley, but in the right deck it can make an opponent hard to eliminate.

**Card Name:**   *Soldevi Excavations*

**Card Type:**   Land

**Card Text:**   When Soldevi Excavations comes into play, sacrifice an untapped island or bury Soldevi Excavations. T: Add 1U to your mana pool. 1, T: Look at the top of your library. You may put that card on the bottom of your library.

**Soldevi Excavations Revealed:** The Soldevi Excavations is a strong addition to blue. It allows a blue player to cycle through his deck until he finds the right card. Among the colored special Alliances lands, the Excavations ranks second only to the Kjeldoran Outpost in effectiveness.

| | |
|---|---|
| **Card Name:** | *Thawing Glaciers* |
| **Card Type:** | Land |
| **Card Text:** | Comes into play tapped. 1, T: Search your library for a basic land and put it into play tapped. This does not count toward your one-land-per-turn limit. Shuffle your library afterwards. At the end of turn, return Thawing Glaciers to owner's hand. |

**Thawing Glaciers Revealed:** Thawing Glaciers has been called the Land Tax of Alliances. The Glaciers is not by any means as strong as Land Tax, but it can give its controller a card advantage without requiring less land than the opponent. The Glaciers allows its controller to draw an extra card (land) once every other turn. I would not recommend playing with more than two of these cards as they do not produce mana themselves, and you cannot use more than two effectively at one time.

# Gold

| | |
|---|---|
| **Card Name:** | *Energy Arc* |
| **Casting Cost:** | W U |
| **Card Type:** | Instant |
| **Card Text:** | Untap any number of target creatures. Those creatures neither deal nor receive damage in combat this turn. |

**Energy Arc Revealed:** The Energy Arc can work well both offensively and defensively. If an opponent attacks, you can use the card as a modified Fog and receive no damage. Also the Energy Arc aids Prodigal Sorcerers and other creatures with special abilities that require them to tap. I do not think that Energy Arc belongs in any tournament-level constructed deck. It might attend well to a sealed or draft format.

| | |
|---|---|
| **Card Name:** | *Lim-Dûl's Paladin* |
| **Casting Cost:** | 2BR |
| **Card Type:** | Summon Paladin (0/3) |
| **Card Text:** | Trample. During your upkeep, choose and discard a card from your hand, or bury Lim-Dûl's Paladin and draw a card. If any creatures are assigned to block it, Lim-Dûl's Paladin gets +6/+3 until end of turn. If Lim-Dûl's Paladin attacks and is not blocked, it deals no damage to defending player this turn and that player loses 4 life. Effects that prevent or redirect damage cannot be used to counter this loss of life. |

**Lim-Dûl's Paladin Revealed:** Lim-Dûl's Paladin is a very strong sealed or draft card but is weak in constructed formats because it is so easy to eliminate. It can be Bolted, Swordsed, Incinerated, Exiled, and basically smashed by any number of anti-creature spells. The Paladin's upkeep cost causes a serious loss of card economy, a deadly penalty in Magic. Discarding cards to maintain a creature debilitates any deck. One nice combination with the Paladin is with Bestial Fury. I witnessed this once in sealed deck play, and no matter what the opposing player chooses to do, he or she takes damage.

| | |
|---|---|
| **Card Name:** | *Lim-Dûl's Vault* |
| **Casting Cost:** | UB |
| **Card Type:** | Instant |
| **Card Text:** | Look at the top five cards of your library. As many times as you choose, you may pay 1 life to put those cards on the bottom of your library and look at the top five cards of your library. Shuffle all but the top five cards of your library; put those five on top of your library in any order. Effects that prevent or redirect damage cannot be used to counter this loss of life. |

**Lim-Dûl's Vault Revealed:** The Lim-Dûl's Vault corresponds to a Demonic Tutor for blue/black. There are four major differences between the Vault and Demonic Tutor. The first is that where the Tutor costs one black and one other, the Vault forces its user to commit to blue. The second major difference is that the Demonic Tutor allows you to draw the card you searched for (meaning that it has no card cost). The Vault, on the other hand, only allows you to put the card on the top of your deck. In addition to its card cost, it also must watch for Millstones or other cards that can affect your deck. The third major difference is that the Vault allows you to rearrange your next five cards, so that you can plan the sequence in which you draw them. Fourth, the Vault can be played as an instant at the end of an opponent's turn. This makes the Vault harder to cast. Because the Vault is an instant, it can produce a very early kill when used with Mirror Universe. A player can "Vault" until he reaches zero life during his upkeep, and switch life with the opponent with the Mirror Universe. This card suits constructed better than sealed deck environments.

| Card Name: | ***Lord of Tresserhorn*** |
|---|---|
| **Casting Cost:** | 1UBR |
| **Card Type:** | Summon Legend (10/4) |
| **Card Text:** | When Lord of Tresserhorn comes into play, pay 2 life and sacrifice two creatures; and target opponent draws two cards. Effects that prevent or redirect damage cannot be used to counter this loss of life. B: Regenerate. |

**Lord of Tresserhorn Revealed:** The Lord of Tresserhorn is not a good creature for constructed decks. Though it is large, too many decks have too many ways to eliminate it. It can be removed from the game with Swords to Plowshares or Exile, buried with Balance and Wrath of God, and stolen with Binding Grasp and Control Magic. When it enters play, you will not only lose two creatures and two life but also supply two more cards to eliminate it. In sealed deck and booster draft, on the other hand, the Lord is very strong. Few ways exist to eliminate it, and it will bludgeon an opponent.

| | |
|---|---|
| **Card Name:** | *Misfortune* |
| **Casting Cost:** | 1BRG |
| **Card Type:** | Sorcery |
| **Card Text:** | Target opponent chooses one: you put a +1/+1 counter on each creature you control and gain 4 life; or you put a -1/-1 counter on each creature that your opponent controls and Misfortune deals 4 damage to him or her. |

**Misfortune Revealed:** Misfortune, like the Lord of Tresserhorn, acclimates better in a sealed or draft environment than in a constructed deck. The main reason is that its cost does not justify its effect. Because your opponent has an option as to how he wants the spell to resolve, its effectiveness founders.

| | |
|---|---|
| **Card Name:** | *Nature's Blessing* |
| **Casting Cost:** | 2WG |
| **Card Type:** | Enchantment |
| **Card Text:** | WG: Choose and discard a card from your hand to have target creature gain banding, first strike, or trample or get a +1/+1 counter. |

**Nature's Blessing Revealed:** Nature's Blessing competes capably in both sealed and constructed deck play. It can give creatures bonuses to boost their power in combat. Also, the Blessing provides a way to make useless cards useful. For example, if an opponent uses a creatureless deck, you can use the Blessing to enhance your own creatures by discarding Swords to Plowshares, Wrath of Gods, and Exiles.

| | |
|---|---|
| **Card Name:** | *Phelddagrif* |
| **Casting Cost:** | 1WUG |
| **Card Type:** | Summon Legend (4/4) |
| **Card Text:** | W: Flying until end of turn. Target opponent gains 2 life. U: Return Phelddagrif to owner's hand. Target opponent may draw a card. G: Trample until end of turn. Put a Hippo token into play under target opponent's control. Treat this token as a 1/1 green creature. |

**Phelddagrif Revealed:** The Phelddagrif is strong in the Type II format, but is very robust in Ice Age/Alliances. In many situations in Type II, many creatures will work better than the Phelddagrif. If you have the colored mana available, the Phelddagrif can come out fairly quickly and once in play is difficult to remove. The greatest attribute of the Phelddagrif is its versatility. The Phelddagrif can be an untouchable flying trampling 4/4 Hippo for four mana. Many compare the Blinking Spirit to the Hippo. One of the major disadvantages of the Hippo is that a Red Blast removes it without any opportunity to return Mr. Phelddagrif to your hand. None of its special abilities provide an opponent with any advantage that offsets the Phelddagrif's ability. If an opponent uses a card to remove the Phelddagrif and you return it to your hand, he nets nothing even though he gets to draw another card. If you make the Phelddagrif flying to attack, you will let your opponent gain two life while dealing four. If you give the Phelddagrif trample, you only give your opponent a 1/1 creature. For the most part, the Phelddagrif is a very strong creature.

| | |
|---|---|
| **Card Name:** | *Surge of Strength* |
| **Casting Cost:** | RG |
| **Card Type:** | Instant |
| **Card Text:** | Choose and discard a red or green card from your hand to have target creature gain trample and get +X/+0 until end of turn, where X is equal to that creature's casting cost. |

**Surge of Strength Revealed:** Surge of Strength supplements any red/green creature deck. This card works best on large creatures like Lhurgoyfs or Scaled Wurms. Many red/green creature decks have problems with regenerating or blinking creatures. The Surge of Strength enables a red/green player to overcome these difficulties. The most serious peril of the Surge lies with an opponent that withholds some form of creature removal, which can result in a serious loss of card economy. If removed, your opponent experiences a three-to-one card advantage (Surge of Strength, creature, and discarded card).

| | |
|---|---|
| **Card Name:** | *Wandering Mage* |
| **Casting Cost:** | WUB |
| **Card Type:** | Summon Cleric (0/3) |
| **Card Text:** | W: Pay 1 life to prevent up to 2 damage to any creature. Effects that prevent or redirect damage cannot be used to counter this loss of life. U: Prevent 1 damage to any Cleric or Wizard. B: Put a -1/-1 counter on target creature you control to prevent up to 2 damage to any player. |

**Wandering Mage Revealed:** At first glance the Wandering Mage seems weak. When this creature is in play, it can salvage Orders of the Ebon Hand or Orders of Leitbur from Lightning Bolts or other direct damage, as well as heal itself. You can put numerous -1/-1 counters on one creature (beyond its power and toughness if done as one effect) to prevent great amounts of damage. Though the Mage is not a candidate for many tournament decks, it is stronger than players expect.

| | |
|---|---|
| **Card Name:** | *Winter's Night* |
| **Casting Cost:** | WRG |
| **Card Type:** | Enchant World |
| **Card Text:** | Whenever a snow-covered land is tapped for mana, it produces one additional mana of the same type and does not untap during its controller's next untap phase. |

**Winter's Night Revealed:** Winter's Night may not be effective, but it makes nice wallpaper. I myself will use it to decorate the study of my recently purchased mansion. But I digress. To begin, its multicolor casting cost makes it unwieldy but there are some advantages it has over the Mana Flare. First, you can use it in a deck with snow-covered lands with the hope that your opponent has none. This can be advantageous in a Jokulhaups deck. After casting a Jokulhaups, both players will have to take time to recover lands. The player with Winter's Night will be able to cast high-cost spells much earlier than the opponent. Mixed in a deck with non-snow- and snow-covered land, Winter's Night can ensure he maintains some mana for the subsequent turn.

# Green

| Card Name: | ***Bounty of the Hunt*** |
|---|---|
| **Casting Cost:** | 3GG |
| **Card Type:** | Instant |
| **Card Text:** | You may remove a green card in your hand from the game instead of paying Bounty of the Hunt's casting cost. Put three +1/+1 counters, distributed any way you choose, on any number of target creatures. Remove these counters at end of turn. |

**Bounty of the Hunt Revealed:** Bounty of the Hunt is not exactly the strongest card in the Alliances set, but could fortify an Ice Age/Alliances small creature deck. Here it serves as a nice counter to Pyroclasym. Of the different "toss" ability Alliances cards, the Bounty is the weakest. Its casting cost is much too high for its effect.

| Card Name: | ***Deadly Insects*** |
|---|---|
| **Casting Cost:** | 4G |
| **Card Type:** | Summon Insect (6/1) |
| **Card Text:** | Cannot be the target of spells or effects. |

**Deadly Insects Revealed:** The Deadly Insects is the best creature to emerge from the Alliances set. The one green in the casting cost allows it to fit into decks with only a tinge of green mana. Though there are some key differences, the Insects resembles the Autumn Willow with its protection from targeted spells. While the Willow is less susceptible to cards like Pyroclasym and Earthquake than the Insects, the Insects is cheaper to cast and deals a greater amount of damage. The Deadly Insects, like the Autumn Willow, works best in decks that deny an opponent his mana resources. Excluding Pyroclasym and Balance, a Deadly Insects requires at least four mana or a blocking creature to remove. When you successfully cast one, I recommend that you fill your mouth with a soft drink, arch your back, bug your eyes out, leer at your opponent, and as you let cola dribble out of your mouth, simultaneously utter the words, "Deeeeaaaaaaddddly Iiiiiinnnnnnsssseecttts," in an elderly and sinister voice.

| | |
|---|---|
| **Card Name:** | *Elvish Bard* |
| **Casting Cost:** | 3GG |
| **Card Type:** | Summon Elf (2/4) |
| **Card Text:** | All creatures able to block Elvish Bard do so. If this forces a creature to block more attackers than allowed, defending player assigns that creature to block as many of those attackers as allowed. |

**Elvish Bard Revealed:** The Elvish Bard has a number of qualities that commend its use. First, the Bard allows its controller to eliminate nuisance creatures like the Deadly Insects. If placed in play early, it can maul an opponent's fast creatures. You can accomplish this by leaving the Bard untapped to block. If an opponent does not attack, then attack with the Bard and force all untapped creatures to block it. The Bard also works well in sealed deck or draft environments. Often in these environments, there are a low number of global creature destruction spells such as Wrath of God, Balance, and Nevinyrral's Disk. This means that in the late game there tends to be an amassing of creatures on either side. Once the Bard enters play, it allows its controller to conduct an attack in which only his Bard will be blocked. This can decide a game if enough damage dealing creatures exist under the attacking player's control.

| Card Name: | *Elvish Ranger* |
| --- | --- |
| Casting Cost: | 2G |
| Card Type: | Summon Elf (4/1) |
| Card Text: | none |

**Elvish Ranger Revealed:** The Ranger is a strong creature in the sealed deck and Ice Age/Alliances environment. Its four points of puissant force makes it a formidable damage dealer. Add it to decks with excessive creature removal to support the Ranger's low toughness: a simple Fyndhorn Elves can eliminate a Ranger. This low toughness damages its use in the Type II environment. Serrated Arrows and Meekstone make it difficult for the Ranger to perform well in the Type II environment.

| Card Name: | *Elvish Spirit Guide* |
| --- | --- |
| Casting Cost: | 2G |
| Card Type: | Summon Spirit (2/2) |
| Card Text: | If Elvish Spirit Guide is in your hand, you may remove it from the game to add G to your mana pool. Play this ability as an interrupt. |

**Elvish Spirit Guide Revealed:** The Spirit Guide is unique in Magic. It is the only card that a player may discard from his hand to produce mana. Along with this interesting ability, it also provides green another source of fast mana. With the Spirit Guide and a couple of Tinder Walls, you can cast a first-turn Balduvian Hordes (but fear the Swords to Plowshares). The Guide also brings a surprise factor. A tapped-out opponent no longer equates with an inability to cast instants. The Guide is strong in Winter Orb/Howling Mine decks where mana is scarce and cards plentiful. Unlike a Dark Ritual, if you happen to draw the Guide in the late game, you can still cast it as a creature.

| Card Name: | *Fyndhorn Druid* |
|---|---|
| **Casting Cost:** | 2G |
| **Card Type:** | Summon Druid (2/2) |
| **Card Text:** | If Fyndhorn Druid is put into the graveyard the same turn it was blocked, gain 4 life. |

**Fyndhorn Druid Revealed:** The Fyndhorn Druid's special ability can prevent an opponent from attacking until he finds some method for removing the Druid. If the Druid is eliminated but manages to kill a creature in combat, it nets its controller four life. In constructed deck environments, the Druid is not very powerful because of the large amount of creature removal. In sealed and draft environments though, the Druid is much stronger. Most opponents will avoid using their limited and precious creature control on a Druid in a non-constructed environment.

| | |
|---|---|
| **Card Name:** | *Gargantuan Gorilla* |
| **Casting Cost:** | 4GGG |
| **Card Type:** | Summon Gorilla (7/7) |
| **Card Text:** | During your upkeep, sacrifice a forest, or bury Gargantuan Gorilla and Gargantuan Gorilla deals 7 damage to you. If you sacrifice a snow-covered forest in this way, Gargantuan Gorilla gains trample until end of turn. T: Gargantuan Gorilla deals an amount of damage equal to its power to any other target creature. That creature deals an amount of damage equal to its power to Gargantuan Gorilla. |

**Gargantuan Gorilla Revealed:** The Gargantuan Gorilla is worth its cost in the Ice Age/Alliances format and might also fit well in some tournament level Type II decks. If used with snow-covered lands, this creature will end games. Blue mages will be unlikely to steal these beasts because they will commonly lack the forests to support them. The major difficulty with the Gorilla is getting it into play. Seven mana is no paltry sum, but if used with cards like Mana Vaults, Dark Rituals, Lumber-jacks, or Tinder Walls, these creatures can enter play in the mid game. Once they are in play, an opponent either eliminates them or, as Snagglepuss says, they exit stage left. Beyond being a major source of damage, the Gorilla adds a much needed element of creature control to green. Once the Gorilla is in play, he can eliminate Erhnams, Vampires, and Angels.

| | |
|---|---|
| **Card Name:** | *Gift of the Woods* |
| **Casting Cost:** | G |
| **Card Type:** | Enchant Creature |
| **Card Text:** | If enchanted creature blocks or is blocked by any creatures, enchanted creature gets +0/+3 until end of turn and you gain 1 life. |

**Gift of the Woods Revealed:** Gift of the Woods might work well in a sealed environment but is an unlikely candidate for constructed deck. It suffers from the same problem that most creature enchantments carry; this will be reiterated throughout the book: if the creature it enchants is removed, the creature's controller suffers a loss of card advantage. If the Gift of the Woods gave a permanent +0/+3 it might be worthwhile because it would take the creature it enchants out of Lightning Bolt range. As it stands, the said creature can easily be eliminated.

| | |
|---|---|
| **Card Name:** | *Gorilla Berserkers* |
| **Casting Cost:** | 3GG |
| **Card Type:** | Summon Gorillas (2/3) |
| **Card Text:** | Trample, rampage: 2. Cannot be blocked by fewer than three creatures. |

**Gorilla Berserkers Revealed:** Another card that rests well with a sealed deck or draft environment. There, it is unlikely it will ever be blocked. If an opponent does dare to throw three creatures in front of the Berserkers, the creature gains an additional six to both power and toughness. In constructed deck, players can easily remove these creatures. A tournament level deck is unlikely to have room for a five-casting-cost creature that is susceptible to one Lightning Bolt.

| | |
|---|---|
| **Card Name:** | *Gorilla Chieftain* |
| **Casting Cost:** | 2GG |
| **Card Type:** | Summon Gorilla (3/3) |
| **Card Text:** | 1G: Regenerate |

**Gorilla Chieftain Revealed:** The Chieftain is green's second regenerating creature, the first being the Yavimaya Gnats. These creatures are well worth their cost. They will fit well in a red/green Nevinyrral's Disk deck, right alongside Uthden Trolls. The Chieftain is still very vulnerable to an Incinerate, and in most cases, a Lightning Bolt when first cast, but otherwise compensates well for its expense. These creatures are large enough that they pose a significant threat offensively and defensively. Two of these creatures together can eliminate an Erhnam Djinn, with only one needing to regenerate. The only great limitation of the Chieftain is the two green in its casting cost. Any deck employing more than one or two of these creatures will need to use green as its primary color.

| | |
|---|---|
| **Card Name:** | *Hail Storm* |
| **Casting Cost:** | 1GG |
| **Card Type:** | Instant |
| **Card Text:** | Hail Storm deals 2 damage to each attacking creature and 1 damage to you and each creature you control. |

**Hail Storm Revealed:** Hail Storm is another addition to green's much-needed creature control. The Storm provides the green mage with the ability to eliminate such problems as Hypnotic Specters, both black and white Orders, Mishra's Factories, and mass small creature attacks. You can avoid the negative side effects of the Storm by not using creatures with toughness less than two. Also the Hail Storm provides another way to make Fungusaurs bigger. I expect to see the majority of all green tournament decks packing at least a couple of Hail Storms in the sideboard.

| | |
|---|---|
| **Card Name:** | *Kaysa* |
| **Casting Cost:** | 3GG |
| **Card Type:** | Summon Legend (2/3) |
| **Card Text:** | All green creatures you control get +1/+1. |

**Kaysa Revealed:** Kaysa is the long-awaited green Crusade. Though a creature, she is a little more durable than first appears. Because she is green she adds her bonus to herself and so comes into play as a 3/4. The disadvantage of Kaysa is that she is a Legend, making it impossible to put more than one in play at a time. Kaysa is strong in many respects. Not only a decent sized creature, she invigorates green creature decks. Additionally, unlike a Crusade, Kaysa only gives her bonus to her controller's green creatures.

| Card Name: | *Nature's Chosen* |
| --- | --- |
| **Casting Cost:** | G |
| **Card Type:** | Enchant Creature |
| **Card Text:** | Play on a creature you control. 0: Untap enchanted creature. Use this ability only during your turn and only once each turn. 0: Tap enchanted creature to untap target artifact, creature, or land. Use this ability only if enchanted creature is white and only once each turn. |

**Nature's Chosen Revealed:** Nature's Chosen is another version of Instill Energy. The Chosen's second ability with white creatures might work well in a Stasis or Winter Orb deck to maintain a source of mana. For the most part, however, Nature's Chosen is a weak card for the same reason most creature enchantments are weak. If the opponent removes the creature it enchants, then there is a loss in card advantage.

| Card Name: | **Nature's Wrath** |
|---|---|
| **Casting Cost:** | 4GG |
| **Card Type:** | Enchantment |
| **Card Text:** | During your upkeep, pay G or bury Nature's Wrath. Whenever a player puts a swamp or black permanent into play, he or she sacrifices a swamp or black permanent. Whenever a player puts an island or a blue permanent into play, he or she sacrifices an island or a blue permanent. |

**Nature's Wrath Revealed:** Nature's Wrath is too expensive for the function it performs. If you manage to cast it, there is a possibility of establishing a lock against a blue or black player via a Wrath or a Jokulhaups followed by a forest. This scenario is pretty unrealistic though. A black deck would more than likely eliminate you before then, and a blue deck would probably just counter both spells.

| Card Name: | **Splintering Wind** |
|---|---|
| **Casting Cost:** | 2GG |
| **Card Type:** | Enchantment |
| **Card Text:** | 2G: Splintering Wind deals 1 damage to target creature. Put a Splinter token into play. Treat this token as a 1/1 green creature with flying and Cumulative Upkeep: G. If this token leaves play, it deals 1 damage to you and to each creature you control. |

**Splintering Wind Revealed:** Splintering Wind is not a card that will not show up in the finals of any major constructed deck tournament. Its expense and drawbacks far outweigh its benefits in constructed deck and are hard to justify in sealed deck environments. If you use the Splintering Wind more than once, you must maintain two token creatures or you and your creatures will suffer two points of damage.

| Card Name: | *Taste of Paradise* |
| --- | --- |
| **Casting Cost:** | 3G |
| **Card Type:** | Sorcery |
| **Card Text:** | Gain 3 life. Gain 3 life for each 1G you pay in addition to the casting cost. |

**Taste of Paradise Revealed:** The Taste of Paradise is a more efficient Stream of Life. The initial costing cost equates to a three-point Stream of Life but subsequently provides its caster three life for every two mana tapped as opposed to the two that a Stream provides. There are few occasions where Stream of Life is preferable. In some sealed environments you may run only a very small amount of green mana, in which case a Stream may provide more life in the late game than the Taste.

| Card Name: | *Tornado* |
| --- | --- |
| **Casting Cost:** | 4G |
| **Card Type:** | Enchantment |

**Card Text:** Cumulative Upkeep: G. 2G: Pay 3 life
for each velocity counter on Tornado.
Destroy target permanent and put a
velocity counter on Tornado. Use this
ability only once each turn. Effects that
prevent or redirect damage cannot be
used to counter this loss of life.

**Tornado Revealed:** For the cost of six life, you can use
Tornado to eliminate three of an opponent's permanents.
Though you cannot support a Tornado for long because
of its cumulative upkeep, it can generate enough removal
to justify its cost. If, for instance, you only have the
mana in play to cast the Tornado, you can still eliminate
two permanents with it over the course of three turns.
There is a high probability that you would draw another
land allowing you to activate the enchantment a third
time. Tornado is a card that I expect to see in a number
of Type II and Alliances/Ice Age tournament decks.

**Card Name:** *Undergrowth*

**Casting Cost:** G

**Card Type:** Instant

**Card Text:** No creatures deal damage in combat
this turn. If you pay 2R in addition to
the casting cost, Undergrowth does not
affect red creatures.

**Undergrowth Revealed:** Many players refer to Undergrowth as the Fog with holes in it. In my humble opinion
this card is about three times as good as Fog in a
green/red deck. Here is an example. If my opponent
attacks me with a pair of pump Knights and I have a pair

of Llanowar Elves in play, I can eliminate both Knights if I have two red and four other mana available (excluding the Elves). This is regardless of whether the Knights are given first strike or not. I would not be surprised to see this card pop up in a constructed tournament deck every once in awhile.

| | |
|---|---|
| **Card Name:** | *Whip Vine* |
| **Casting Cost:** | 2G |
| **Card Type:** | Summon Wall (1/4) |
| **Card Text:** | Can block creatures with flying. You may choose not to untap Whip Vine during your untap phase. T: Tap target creature with flying blocked by Whip Vine. That creature does not untap during its controller's untap phase as long as Whip Vine remains tapped. |

**Whip Vine Revealed:** The Whip Vine provides green with more defense against flying creatures. Generally, I do not like walls in constructed deck environments. If you play against a creatureless deck, walls are useless. This is a much better card in sealed and draft decks where creatureless decks simply do not exist. One important feature that escapes most people about the Whip Vine is that after it blocks a creature with flying, it can tap that creature at any time. So if you block a Hypnotic Specter and three turns later an opponent plays a Feast of the Unicorn, the Whip Vine can tap it. This can also be an asset when conducting an attack. Many opponents will forget that the Whip Vine can tap the creature regardless of when it was blocked. Consider the following: If you were to attack with an Elvish Hunter and an opponent blocked with an Abyssal Specter that was blocked several turns earlier by the Whip Vine, the Vine can tap the Specter after the blocking is declared. This would prevent the Specter from dealing damage, but not from receiving it. Though the Vine would not fit in any constructed deck, it would support most sealed decks.

| | |
|---|---|
| **Card Name:** | *Yavimaya Ancients* |
| **Casting Cost:** | 3GG |
| **Card Type:** | Summon Treefolk (2/7) |
| **Card Text:** | G: +1/-2 until end of turn. |

**Yavimaya Ancients Revealed:** The Ancients are a better alternative to the Ironroot Treefolk. Unlike the Ironroot Treefolk, the Ancients can transform to a 5/1 creature for only three mana. The Ancients are better defensive and offensive creatures than their Ironroot counterparts.

| | |
|---|---|
| **Card Name:** | *Yavimaya Ants* |
| **Casting Cost:** | 2GG |
| **Card Type:** | Summon Swarm (5/1) |
| **Card Text:** | Trample. Cumulative Upkeep: GG. Yavimaya Ants can attack the turn it comes into play on your side. |

**Yavimaya Ants Revealed:** One player comparison described the Yavimaya Ants as "the Ball Lightning that hangs around." This card works well in decks that use an intense level of damage. Also, these creatures are more likely to provide an economic card advantage than Ball Lightnings. This is because an opponent is more likely to block the Ants to prevent them from striking a second time. Even if blocked, this card is likely to deal damage while removing the creature, making its controller the victor of such an exchange.

# Red

| | |
|---|---|
| **Card Name:** | *Agent of Stromgald* |
| **Casting Cost:** | R |
| **Card Type:** | Summon Knight (1/1) |
| **Card Text:** | R: Add B to your mana pool. Play this ability as an interrupt. |

**Agent of Stromgald Revealed:** The Agent makes it easier for black/red players to play with a higher concentration of red spells and still use black cards that have two black in their cost. The Agent used in conjunction with Initiates of the Ebon Hand can maximize the flexibility of a player's land. Also, the Agent allows a black player to use Drain Life in a deck with a high concentration of red mana, another example of the versatility it allows.

| | |
|---|---|
| **Card Name:** | *Balduvian Horde* |
| **Casting Cost:** | 2RR |
| **Card Type:** | Summon Barbarians (5/5) |
| **Card Text:** | When Balduvian Horde comes into play, discard a card at random from your hand or bury Balduvian Horde. |

**Balduvian Horde Revealed:** The Horde undoubtedly ranks as the most overrated creature in the Alliances set. Many people have compared it to the Juzam Djinn, but there are several deficiencies with the Horde that distinguish the Juzam as a better creature. First the Juzam is black, making it immune to Terror, Dark Banishing, and Feast or Famine. Second, the Juzam takes one card to cast on the second turn (Dark Ritual). The Horde extinguishes two cards to cast on the second turn (Tinder Wall plus a card lost at random). Red also lacks any fast mana of its own, compelling you to look to another color like black or green to get the Horde out quickly. If a Horde is cast on the second turn and Sword-sed, then your opponent experiences a three-to-one card advantage. The Hordes is a good creature, but comparisons with the Juzam should cease.

| | |
|---|---|
| **Card Name:** | ***Balduvian War-Makers*** |
| **Casting Cost:** | 4R |
| **Card Type:** | Summon Barbarians (3/3) |
| **Card Text:** | Rampage: 1. Balduvian War-Makers can attack the turn it comes into play on your side. |

**Balduvian War-Makers Revealed:** The War-Makers falls short of consideration as a tournament worthy card for constructed deck play. For virtually the same casting cost, you can play an Erron the Relentless. The War-Makers are Boltable and expensive, and their rampage ability is virtually meaningless. I would consider these creatures for booster draft or sealed deck, but they would never appear in a constructed deck.

| | |
|---|---|
| **Card Name:** | ***Bestial Fury*** |
| **Casting Cost:** | 2R |
| **Card Type:** | Enchant Creature |

**Card Text:**   Draw a card at the beginning of the upkeep of the turn after Bestial Fury comes into play. If enchanted creature attacks and is blocked, it gains trample and gets +4/+0 until end of turn.

**Bestial Fury Revealed:** Simply stated, Bestial Fury is the best creature enchantment in Magic. Not only does it give a creature trample and +4/0, it is a cantrip and has no card cost. This card might as well give the creature it enchants trample because trample is only effective if a creature is blocked. This card will appear in a number of tournament level decks. It works particularly well on large creatures like the Lhurgoyf. Bestial Fury also serves as an excellent counter to nuisances like Blinking Spirits, Uthden Trolls, and Willow the Wisps.

**Card Name:**   *Burnout*

**Casting Cost:**   1R

**Card Type:**   Interrupt

**Card Text:**   Counter target spell if it is blue. Draw a card at the beginning of the next turn's upkeep.

**Burnout Revealed:** Burnout is not a bad card, but it pales in comparison to the Red Elemental Blast, and will not eliminate blue permanents or counter cards like Ancestral Recall or Library of Lat-Nam. You should note that it is much stronger in Type II than in Type I because of the low number of powerful blue instants and sorceries.

| Card Name: | ***Chaos Harlequin*** |
|---|---|
| **Casting Cost:** | 2RR |
| **Card Type:** | Summon Harlequin (2/4) |
| **Card Text:** | R: Remove the top card of your library from the game. If that card is a land, Chaos Harlequin gets -4/-0 until end of turn; otherwise, Chaos Harlequin gets +2/+0 until end of turn. |

**Chaos Harlequin Revealed:** The Chaos Harlequin functions much better as a Type II card than an Ice Age/Alliances card. In Type II, it can be used with the Sylvan Library to allow you to cycle through your deck and ensure that the Harlequin is large when it attacks. You can activate the Harlequin at any time, and this ability could remove excess land during an opponent's end phase. Though the use of the Library with the Harlequin is a card combination, each of the cards is effective independently.

| Card Name: | ***Death Spark*** |
|---|---|
| **Casting Cost:** | R |
| **Card Type:** | Instant |
| **Card Text:** | Death Spark deals 1 damage to target creature or player. At the end of your upkeep, if Death Spark is in your graveyard with a creature card directly above it, you may pay 1 to put Death Spark into your hand. |

**Death Spark Revealed:** Because of its special ability, the Death Spark works best in creature decks. To ensure that you retrieve the Spark, cast it each time an opponent removes a creature from play to the graveyard. This will ensure that a creature will be above it since affects resolve in last-in, first-out order (LIFO) within a spell stack. The Spark works much better as an anti-creature spell than as a spell to target an opponent. It is best employed when used to remove Elves and Orders. Sometimes the Spark can provide the one point of damage to eliminate a large creature, as in the case of two Erhnams dealing damage to one another.

| | |
|---|---|
| **Card Name:** | *Enslaved Scout* |
| **Casting Cost:** | 2R |
| **Card Type:** | Summon Goblin (2/2) |
| **Card Text:** | 2: Mountainwalk until end of turn. |

**Enslaved Scout Revealed:** The Enslaved Scout crushes skulls in a sealed deck or draft environment! Most decks in the sealed and draft environment will add at least a touch of red to utilize some direct damage. One of the keys to success in these environments is breaking the stalemate of creature standoffs. The Scout's mountain-walking ability allows a player to break these standoffs. In contrast, in constructed deck play there is little room for creatures like the Scout. There are many more versatile creatures that can fill that slot. One interesting feature of the Scout is that its controller can give it mountainwalk several times. This allows its controller to sink mana into it to avoid Drain Power, Power Surge, or other similar damage.

| | |
|---|---|
| **Card Name:** | *Gorilla Shaman* |
| **Casting Cost:** | R |
| **Card Type:** | Summon Gorilla (1/1) |
| **Card Text:** | XX1: Destroy target non-creature artifact with casting cost equal to X. |

**Gorilla Shaman Revealed:** The Gorilla Shaman makes an excellent Type I card. It allows its controller to eliminate zero casting cost artifacts such as Moxes for only one mana. This ability lends itself on the turn the Shaman is cast, as well as multiple times on the same turn. The Shaman is also a 1/1 creature for only one mana. This makes it worthwhile in itself. The Shaman is a bit more difficult to use, however, in the Type II environment where zero cost artifacts are less abundant. In order to eliminate an Icy Manipulator, the Shaman's controller needs nine mana available. Nonetheless, the Shaman still smashes Zuran Orbs, Jeweled Amulets, Fountains of Youth, Black Vises, and Ivory Towers.

| | |
|---|---|
| **Card Name:** | *Gorilla War Cry* |
| **Casting Cost:** | 1R |
| **Card Type:** | Instant |
| **Card Text:** | Attacking creatures cannot be blocked by only one creature this turn. Play only during combat before defense is chosen. |

**Gorilla War Cry Revealed:** Consider the War Cry doody. For one more mana its caster could have Goblin War Drums which could be used for multiple turns. But there are two advantages that the War Cry has over the Drums. The first is that the War Cry cannot be disenchanted, causing the attacking creatures to lose their ability. Second, the War Cry can surprise during combat. This noted, I still do not expect to ever see the War Cry used in a tournament-level constructed deck.

| | |
|---|---|
| **Card Name:** | *Guerrilla Tactics* |
| **Casting Cost:** | 1R |
| **Card Type:** | Instant |
| **Card Text:** | Guerrilla Tactics deals 2 damage to target creature or player. If a spell or effect controlled by an opponent causes you to discard Guerrilla Tactics from your hand, reveal Guerrilla Tactics to all players and it deals 4 damage to target creature or player. |

**Guerrilla Tactics Revealed:** Guerrilla Tactics adds a much needed anti-hand destruction element to red and to the Magic environment in general. Though the Guerrilla Tactics is no remedy for the Hymn to Tourach, it will aid in its downfall. Guerrilla Tactics is intended as a natural companion to decks with a large amount of other red instants like Lightning Bolts and Incinerates. If you happen to have four cards in hand, two of which are Lightning Bolts and two which are Tactics, you can deal fourteen points of damage to an opponent casting a Hymn to Tourach. The Tactics is one of the solid additions Alliances provides for red.

| Card Name: | *Omen of Fire* |
| --- | --- |
| Casting Cost: | 3RR |
| Card Type: | Instant |
| Card Text: | Return all islands to their owners' hands. Each player sacrifices a plains or a white permanent for each white permanent he or she controls. |

**Omen of Fire Revealed:** The Omen of Fire is stronger against a blue deck than against a white deck. Against blue, you can cast the Omen at the end of an opponent's turn, forcing him to retrieve the majority of his blue sources of mana. This would force an opponent to either counter the Omen or allow an opponent to cast without a great fear of counter magic. In the case of white, I largely prefer the Anarchy, but the Omen is not a bad substitute.

| Card Name: | *Pillage* |
| --- | --- |
| Casting Cost: | 1RR |
| Card Type: | Sorcery |
| Card Text: | Bury target artifact or land. |

**Pillage Revealed:** The Pillage belongs in any deck with enough red mana sources. Its versatility ensures that it will always be a useful card in both the late and early game. The Pillage bestows red the ability to produce a straight red Type II land destruction deck. A player can now use four Pillage, four Orcish Mines, four Stone Rains, four Strip Mines, four Fissures and four Conquers. This excellent card will become almost as common as Disenchant in red Type II decks.

| | |
|---|---|
| **Card Name:** | *Primitive Justice* |
| **Casting Cost:** | 1R |
| **Card Type:** | Sorcery |
| **Card Text:** | Destroy target artifact. Destroy a target artifact for each 1R you pay in addition to the casting cost. Destroy a target artifact and gain 1 life for each 1G you pay in addition to the casting cost. |

**Primitive Justice Revealed:** Also known as the "super Shatter," Primitive Justice supplies a much needed element of mass artifact destruction to Type II. Primitive Justice is likely to replace Shatter in every red deck. The only advantage that Shatter enjoys over the Primitive Justice is that Shatter is cast as an instant. The greatest advantage this gives is in the case of a Winter Orb/Icy Manipulator lock. In that case, an instant recommends itself since you can use it with the mana available during your upkeep. The Primitive Justice is a sorcery and you may not cast it during your upkeep.

| | |
|---|---|
| **Card Name:** | *Pyrokinesis* |
| **Casting Cost:** | 4RR |
| **Card Type:** | Instant |
| **Card Text:** | You may remove a red card in your hand from the game instead of paying Pyrokinesis's casting cost. Pyrokinesis deals 4 damage, divided any way you choose among any number of target creatures. |

**Pyrokinesis Revealed:** Pyrokinesis ranks with Force of Will as one of the better discard or "toss" spells added to the Alliances set. Often with Pyrokinesis you can eliminate multiple creatures, improving your card advantage. Pyrokinesis is a welcome addition to any anti-hand destruction deck. If an opponent Hymns you and you happen to have a Pyrokinesis in hand along with a red card and two Guerrilla Tactics, you can eliminate an opponent's creatures and deal eight points of damage to him or her.

| | |
|---|---|
| **Card Name:** | *Rogue Skycaptain* |
| **Casting Cost:** | 2R |
| **Card Type:** | Summon Mercenary (3/4) |
| **Card Text:** | Flying. At the beginning of you upkeep, put a wage counter on Rogue Skycaptain. During your upkeep, pay 2 for each wage counter on Rogue Skycaptain, or remove all wage counters from Rogue Skycaptain and target opponent gains control of Rogue Skycaptain. |

**Rouge Skycaptain Revealed:** At first glance the Rouge Skycaptain appears very difficult to use effectively. One way to exploit the Skycaptain is to supplement it with land destruction. If your opponent can never keep more than a few lands in play at a time, then he will have difficulty paying the Skycaptain's upkeep cost. Another way to use the Captain is with C.O.P. Red in the standard deck. The Skycaptain possesses some merit, but does not fit in every red deck.

| Card Name: | ***Soldier of Fortune*** |
|---|---|
| **Casting Cost:** | R |
| **Card Type:** | Summon Mercenary (1/1) |
| **Card Text:** | RT: Target player shuffles his or her library. |

**Soldier of Fortune Revealed:** The Soldier of Fortune works well in any deck in which you can look at your cards before you draw them. Decks with Sylvan Library, Orcish Spies, or Field of Dreams operate well with the Soldier of Fortune. Also, the Soldevi Digger can work well with the Soldier because it will allow its controller to retrieve his or her spells, reshuffle the library, and thus increase the possibility of drawing those recycled spells.

| Card Name: | ***Storm Shaman*** |
|---|---|
| **Casting Cost:** | 2R |
| **Card Type:** | Summon Cleric (0/4) |
| **Card Text:** | R: +1/+0 until end of turn. |

**Storm Shaman Revealed:** Storm Shaman translates as the Frozen Shade for red. Shaman is actually stronger than a Frozen Shade because it is less susceptible to Lightning Bolts, and it also complements cards like Meekstone or Dwarven Warriors. With a Meekstone out, the Shaman can swell to an offensive size larger than two and still untap, while an opponent's large creatures will remain tapped if they ever tap to attack. With the Dwarven Warrior, a player can make the Shaman unblockable and then boost its power. These enlightening thoughts aside, I do not believe that the Shaman will

**58**

become a common feature in many tournament-level constructed decks, but it will serve as a very powerful tool for dealing damage in a draft or sealed deck.

| | |
|---|---|
| **Card Name:** | ***Varchild's Crusader*** |
| **Casting Cost:** | 3R |
| **Card Type:** | Summon Knight (3/2) |
| **Card Text:** | 0: Varchild's Crusader cannot be blocked except by walls this turn. Bury Varchild's Crusader at the end of turn. |

**Varchild's Crusader Revealed:** The Varchild's Crusader is not a very strong creature. Four mana is too much to pay for a 3/2 creature. Its special ability is a nice feature, but it does not offset the expense. This creature may appear in a few draft or sealed decks, but I do not believe it will arise in any constructed-deck environment.

| | |
|---|---|
| **Card Name:** | ***Varchild's War-Riders*** |
| **Casting Cost:** | 1R |
| **Card Type:** | Summon War-Riders (3/4) |
| **Card Text:** | Trample, rampage: 1. Cumulative Upkeep: Put a survivor token into play under target opponent's control. Treat this token as a 1/1 red creature. |

**Varchild's War-Riders Revealed:** The Varchild's War-Riders takes a close second only to the Kird Ape in the category of cards that provide high power and toughness relative to their casting cost. The War-Riders is not an easy creature to add to a deck. The side effect of its up-keep can severely diminish its caster's life total. In order to use the War-Riders effectively, a deck must be built around it. One option is to use cards like Earthquake or Pyroclasym to eliminate the Survivor tokens. This is only a temporary solution though, because the War-Riders will just produce more during the next turn's upkeep. An obvious but important point to remember is that you do not have to pay the upkeep and it will simply be buried. Another strategy is to use the card Withering Wisps or Pestilence to clear the playing area before launching an attack. Smoke can also prevent repeated attacks from to-ken creatures. In any case, these are not creatures that accompany any deck with red in it. Carefully construct a deck around this dangerous but potentially useful card.

| Card Name: | *Veteran's Voice* |
|---|---|
| Casting Cost: | R |
| Card Type: | Enchant Creature |
| Card Text: | Play on a creature you control. 0: Tap enchanted creature to give any other target creature +2/+1 until end of turn. |

**Veteran's Voice Revealed:** Lost card economy prevents yet another creature enchantment from the possibility of use in constructed deck environment, although in a sealed or draft environment, Veteran's Voice can serve as a minor asset. In that environment it can allow you to save a creature during combat or deal slightly more damage; it certainly would not constitute a first pick, but might serve as a nice late addition.

# Black

| | |
|---|---|
| **Card Name:** | *Balduvian Dead* |
| **Casting Cost:** | 3B |
| **Card Type:** | Summon Zombies (2/3) |
| **Card Text:** | 2R: Remove target summon card in your graveyard from the game to put a Graveborn token into play. Treat this token as a 3/1 black and red creature that can attack the turn it comes into play. Bury Graveborn token at end of turn. |

**Balduvian Dead Revealed:** One black and three other is expensive for a 2/3 creature, but the Balduvian Dead's special ability is relatively powerful. If used in a deck with a high concentration of creatures, the Balduvian Dead could allow its caster to swamp an opponent after the initial threat of early creatures has been removed. This card also has defensive merit. A player could use two Graveborn tokens to kill an attacking Erhnam or even an Orgg. You might use a Skull Catapult with these creatures to turn them into expensive Lightning Bolts. The major drawback of the Dead is its susceptibility to Lightning Bolts.

| | |
|---|---|
| **Card Name:** | *Casting of Bones* |
| **Casting Cost:** | 2B |
| **Card Type:** | Enchant Creature |
| **Card Text:** | If enchanted creature is put into the graveyard, draw three cards. Choose and discard one of those cards. |

**Casting of Bones Revealed:** The major deficiency with creature enchantments is that when an opponent removes one of your creatures with a single card, he enjoys a card count advantage. Casting of Bones nullifies this advantage, but achieves nothing else. It allows its caster to cycle through his deck faster, given that the creature it enchants slides to the graveyard. If the creature it enchants is removed from the game, it nullifies that advantage. Thus, the best use for this card would be on creatures with protection from white. Because Swords to Plowshares is the most widely used card to remove a creature from the game, creatures with protection from white could avoid this obstacle. It allows the creature's controller to effectively turn that creature into a cantrip. If the creature dies, the caster gains the advantage of card replacement.

| | |
|---|---|
| **Card Name:** | *Contagion* |
| **Casting Cost:** | 3BB |
| **Card Type:** | Instant |
| **Card Text:** | You may pay 1 life and remove a black card in your hand from the game instead of paying Contagion's casting cost. Effects that prevent or redirect damage cannot be used to counter this loss of life. Put two -2/-1 counters, distributed any way you choose, on any number of target creatures. |

**Contagion Revealed:** Next to Bounty of the Hunt, Contagion is the weakest of the new optional discard spells. Its ability is relatively weak in the early game, since there are few early non-protection from black creatures that black has to fear. Like Bounty of the Hunt, this card is most useful during the attack phase. An opponent is likely to make the assumption that you cannot effect combat while you have no mana available. With Contagion, a Hypnotic Specter could eliminate a Serra Angel. This card is best when used with creatures that gain a benefit when they eliminate a blocker, like Vampire. Often a late game Dark Ritual can be used for the card cost that Contagion requires.

| | |
|---|---|
| **Card Name:** | *Diseased Vermin* |
| **Casting Cost:** | 2B |
| **Card Type:** | Summon Rats (1/1) |
| **Card Text:** | During your upkeep, Diseased Vermin deals 1 damage to a single target opponent it has previously damaged for each infection counter on Diseased Vermin. If Diseased Vermin damages a player in combat, put an infection counter on it. |

**Diseased Vermin Revealed:** The Diseased Vermin will join the famed category of "lightning rod," where its brother the Hypnotic Specter already resides. If this creature becomes unblockable, it requires six turns to kill an opponent. The Vermin work well with cards like Dwarven Warriors, Joven's Tools, and Tawnos's Wand. I do not foresee this card utilized in tournament-level decks, but it would be very strong in a sealed deck environment where anti-creature spells are less common.

| Card Name: | ***Dystopia*** |
|---|---|
| **Casting Cost:** | 1BB |
| **Card Type:** | Enchantment |
| **Card Text:** | Cumulative Upkeep: 1 life. During each player's upkeep, if that player controls any green or white permanents, he or she sacrifices a green or white permanent. |

**Dystopia Revealed:** Question: What were they thinking? This single card makes black much more formidable. It gives black the ability to remove C.O.P. Black, Order of Leitbur, Whirling Dervish, Karma, and Life Force. Dystopia is a must for the sideboard of any all-black deck. It is likely to take the place of slots normally reserved for Gloom or Death Grip. Expect this card in the Type II environment.

| Card Name: | ***Fatal Lore*** |
|---|---|
| **Casting Cost:** | 2BB |
| **Card Type:** | Sorcery |
| **Card Text:** | Target opponent chooses one: you draw three cards; or you choose and bury up to two target creatures that opponent controls and he or she draws up to three cards. |

**Fatal Lore Revealed:** This card's utility is severely restricted. I would not consider starting this card in the regular deck. Against creatureless decks, this card is meaningless. It will sit in your hand as dead weight. If you dare cast it while an opponent has no creatures in play, he will take the second option and allow you to remove "up to" two creatures and draw three cards. I prefer Ashes to Ashes over this card since its penalty is less detrimental and it is slightly cheaper.

| | |
|---|---|
| **Card Name:** | *Feast or Famine* |
| **Casting Cost:** | 3B |
| **Card Type:** | Instant |
| **Card Text:** | Bury target non-black, non-artifact creature or put a Zombie token into play. Treat this token as a 2/2 black creature. |

**Feast or Famine Revealed:** This card is versatile and is a worthy addition to black. Though it has a higher casting cost than Terror, it is more likely to be found in the regular deck of all-black decks. If an all-black deck faces another all-black deck, Terror is a useless card. Feast or Famine, however, provides its opponent an instant 2/2 creature that can block a creature to prevent a death blow or simply add to a deck's offense. This is particularly effective because an opponent is not likely to consider the possibility of an instant creature. If an opponent's life total is low, he would not be likely to attack with an opponent's creature in play. But if you have no creatures in play, an opponent will frequently continue his offensive, leaving himself with no blockers. A Feast or Famine token creature cast during an opponent's end phase can avoid a Wrath of God or Fireball and possibly supply a surprise victory.

| | |
|---|---|
| **Card Name:** | *Fevered Strength* |
| **Casting Cost:** | 2B |
| **Card Type:** | Instant |
| **Card Text:** | Target creature gets +2/+0 until end of turn. Draw a card at the beginning of the next turn's upkeep. |

**Fevered Strength Revealed:** Fevered Strength offers black an excellent cantrip. It allows its caster to deal an extra two points of damage with no card cost. Consider it with first strike creatures like Black Knights: an unsuspecting Vampire assigned as a blocker becomes the victim of a Knight targeted by Fevered Strength.

| | |
|---|---|
| **Card Name:** | *Insidious Bookworms* |
| **Casting Cost:** | B |
| **Card Type:** | Summon Worms (1/1) |
| **Card Text:** | 1B: Target player discards a card at random from his or her hand. Use this ability only when Insidious Bookworms is put into the graveyard from play. You cannot spend more than 1B in this way each turn. |

**Insidious Bookworms Revealed:** This card is a nice addition to black's hand destruction ability. First, this card only costs one black, meaning it is useful in the early game. If an opponent plays a Savannah Lion and you manage to draw your Bookworms, not only can you nullify the threat of the Lion attacking, but you can also force the opponent to lose a card at random. There are a number of combinations you can use to increase this card's effectiveness, such as Skull Catapult and Enduring Renewal. These combinations will allow you to eliminate your opponent's hand, and eventually, your opponent.

| | |
|---|---|
| **Card Name:** | *Keeper of Tresserhorn* |
| **Casting Cost:** | 5B |
| **Card Type:** | Summon Keeper (6/6) |
| **Card Text:** | If Keeper of Tresserhorn attacks and is not blocked, it deals no damage to defending player this turn and that player loses 2 life. Effects that prevent or redirect damage cannot be used to counter this loss of life. |

**Keeper of Tresserhorn Revealed:** The Keeper of Tresserhorn is not a particularly strong creature. While its power and toughness are high relative to its casting cost, the Keeper's special ability is as much a hindrance as a boon. The obvious major advantage of the Keeper's special ability is its immunity to a C.O.P. Black. However, cards like Dystopia and Ghostly Flame are much more effective at overcoming C.O.P.s, and cost considerably less.

| | |
|---|---|
| **Card Name:** | ***Krovikan Horror*** |
| **Casting Cost:** | 3B |
| **Card Type:** | Summon Horror (2/2) |
| **Card Text:** | At the end of any turn, if Krovikan Horror is in your graveyard with a summon card directly above it, you may put Krovikan Horror into your hand. 1: Sacrifice a creature to have Krovikan Horror deal 1 damage to target creature or player. |

**Krovikan Horror Revealed:** At first glance these creatures appear worthless and weak. But if used in multiples, you might categorize them as the Blinking Spirit for black. With two in play, you can always block an attacker and recast on the next turn. In some respects, the Horror is stronger than the Blinking Spirit because you actually let damage resolve with the Horror. This card is weaker than the Spirit against decks that use Tormod's Crypt, but remains strong nonetheless. There are some combinations that you can use the Horror with to increase its potency. If you have four Nether Shadows in your graveyard, during your upkeep you can use the Horror's ability to deal as much damage as you have mana sources available. The Horror is very difficult to eliminate. One way to keep an opponent from retrieving his Horror is to remove it and then remove a permanent after the stack resolves. This becomes increasingly more difficult with multiple Horrors in play, as they can use their special ability to maintain a creature above them.

| Card Name: | ***Krovikan Plague*** |
|---|---|
| Casting Cost: | 2B |
| Card Type: | Enchant Creature |
| Card Text: | Play on a non-wall creature you control. Draw a card at the beginning of the upkeep of the turn after Krovikan Plague comes into play. 0: Tap enchanted creature to have Krovikan Plague deal 1 damage to target creature or player. Put a -0/-1 counter on enchanted creature. |

**Krovikan Plague Revealed:** The Krovikan Plague is another of the cantrips added to the Alliances set. This card could fortify cards like Dancing Scimitars or any other non-wall creature with a high toughness. Because the card is a cantrip, there is no risk of lost card economy, and it might also assist in removing small creatures. Its benefits aside, however, do not expect this card to appear in many tournament-level decks.

| Card Name: | ***Lim-Dûl's High Guard*** |
|---|---|
| Casting Cost: | 1BB |
| Card Type: | Summon Skeleton (2/1) |
| Card Text: | First strike. 1B: Regenerate. |

**Lim-Dûl's High Guard Revealed:** Lim-Dûl's High Guard is one of the best creatures to come out of the Alliances set. It works well with Necropotence Hymn Disk decks, as well as Nevinyrral's Disk. It has the ability to kill an opponent's Orders of the Ebon Hand or Knights of

Stromgald and survive. It also regenerates after Disks detonate. However, Serrated Arrows and Incinerate easily eliminate it.

| Card Name: | *Misinformation* |
| --- | --- |
| **Casting Cost:** | B |
| **Card Type:** | Instant |
| **Card Text:** | Put up to three target cards from an opponent's graveyard on top of his or her library in any order. |

**Misinformation Revealed:** Misinformation will be a very strong card in resource denial decks. Decks that use any sort of land destruction will be able to take advantage of this card, such as in Jokulhaups decks. A player can cast a Jokulhaups, and then cast Misinformation to force his opponent to draw non-land cards for three turns. If the card is used with one-shot land destruction (Stone Rain, Strip Mines, etc.) and Hymn to Tourach, you can ensure an opponent draws discarded spells and not land. Even without resource denial, Misinformation demonstrates strength in the late game. You can allow an opponent to draw anti-artifact spells while your creatures pummel them. Misinformation will appear in many tournament-level decks.

| Card Name: | ***Phantasmal Fiend*** |
|---|---|
| Casting Cost: | 3B |
| Card Type: | Summon Phantasm (1/5) |
| Card Text: | B: +1/-1 until end of turn. 1U: Switch Phantasmal Fiend's power and toughness until end of turn. Effects that alter Phantasmal Fiend's power alter its toughness instead, and vice versa. |

**Phantasmal Fiend Revealed:** This creature provides incentive for more players to play with blue/black. Its special ability makes it a strong asset with cards like Dwarven Warriors, Meekstone, or Tawnos's Wand. The Fiend possesses both excellent defensive and offensive qualities. Defensively, it is large enough to block an Erhnam Djinn and survive. The Fiend is most effective when its controller has two blue and two other sources of mana available. This way, the Fiend's controller can attack and activate its special ability, transforming it to a 5/1 without fear of an opponent Bolting it, while dealing a skull-crushing blow. If an opponent casts a Bolt, the controller can swap its power and toughness once again, making it a 1/5 and effectively countering the Bolt.

| Card Name: | ***Phyrexian Boon*** |
|---|---|
| Casting Cost: | 2B |
| Card Type: | Enchant Creature |
| Card Text: | As long as enchanted creature is black, it gets +2/+1; otherwise it gets -1/-2. |

**Phyrexian Boon Revealed:** The Phyrexian Boon's value rests in its versatility. This card can be more effective than Weakness in removing a troublesome creature. For example, if Weakness is cast on an Uthden Troll, the Troll becomes a 0/1 regenerator. But if the Boon enchants the Troll, it dies. Backed up with a Lightning Bolt or Incinerate, the Boon also removes Erhnams. Phyrexian Boon can be used in the main deck of any creature deck without fear of it being useless. If an opponent has no creature to remove it can be used to enhance one of your own.

| Card Name: | *Ritual of the Machine* |
|---|---|
| **Casting Cost:** | 2BB |
| **Card Type:** | Sorcery |
| **Card Text:** | Sacrifice a creature to gain control of target non-black, non-artifact creature. |

**Ritual of the Machine Revealed:** Some refer to Ritual of the Machine as black's Control Magic. The comparison is not completely accurate, as the Ritual differs from Control Magic in a couple of ways. The first and most obvious distinction between the two is that the Ritual's caster must sacrifice a creature upon casting. Thus, the Ritual does not provide the card advantage of Control Magic, although this does not necessarily make the Ritual inferior to Control Magic. Unlike the enchantment Control Magic, the Ritual of the Machine is a sorcery. The relevance of this is that once the caster steals the creature, it cannot be retaken by its original owner with some form of enchantment removal. The Ritual can assist creatures like Ashen Ghouls, Nether Shadows, and

Insidious Bookworms. This is because there is some benefit to sacrificing those creatures to the graveyard.

| Card Name: | ***Soldevi Adnate*** |
|---|---|
| **Casting Cost:** | 1B |
| **Card Type:** | Summon Cleric (1/2) |
| **Card Text:** | T: Sacrifice a black or artifact creature to add an amount of B equal to that creature's casting cost to your mana pool. Play this ability as an interrupt. |

**Soldevi Adnate Revealed:** The Soldevi Adnate is the same creature as the Priest of Yogmath from the Antiquities set. The Adnate operates well with cards like Drain Life and Fireball. A player may achieve a quicker kill with the Adnate, making it a good selection for use in Type I with Su-Chi. Assuming you have the mana to cast the Su-Chi, you can cast a 13-point Fireball. Overall, the Adnate is a balanced creature: it allows its caster to take advantage of its special effect and also possesses a reasonable cost relative to its power and toughness.

| Card Name: | ***Stench of Decay*** |
|---|---|
| **Casting Cost:** | 1BB |
| **Card Type:** | Instant |
| **Card Text:** | All non-artifact creatures get -1/-1 until end of turn. |

**Stench of Decay Revealed:** The Stench of Decay contributes to black's pool of anti-creature defense. It can eliminate a Dervish, Order of Leitbur, or Order of the White Shield because the Stench of Decay does not target. I doubt this card will achieve popularity, as it will kill its caster's creatures with a one toughness as well as an opponent's creatures.

| | |
|---|---|
| **Card Name:** | *Stromgald Spy* |
| **Casting Cost:** | 3B |
| **Card Type:** | Summon Spy (2/4) |
| **Card Text:** | If Stromgald Spy attacks and is not blocked, you may choose to have it deal no damage to defending player this turn. If you do so, defending player must play with his or her hand face up on the table until Stromgald Spy leaves play. |

**Stromgald Spy Revealed:** The Stromgald Spy is a very powerful creature because of its ability. To know what an opponent has in his hand is powerful enough independently. You know when he or she has a Counterspell, Giant Growth, or some other card that could thwart your plan of attack. Often you must guess what an opponent holds in his hand. This card eliminates variables and will aid in making the proper play. One black and three other is not unreasonable for a 2/4 creature with a special ability. The Spy constitutes a nice addition to black's creature pool.

| Card Name: | *Swamp Mosquito* |
|---|---|
| **Casting Cost:** | 1B |
| **Card Type:** | Summon Mosquito (0/1) |
| **Card Text:** | Flying. If Swamp Mosquito attacks and is not blocked, defending player gets a poison counter. If a player has ten or more poison counters, he or she loses the game. |

**Swamp Mosquito Revealed:** The Swamp Mosquito is the first creature that gives poison counters and actually does so somewhat effectively. As a flyer, it is much more difficult to block than its Viper or Scorpion counterparts. Additionally, some advantages exist to using poison counters instead of dealing damage. First, an opponent cannot prevent poison counters with a Circle of Protection. Second, you only require ten poison counters to kill an opponent, which correlates to two points of damage. Cards like the Ivory Tower and Zuran Orb are meaningless when a deck seeks victory by dealing poison counters. At the moment, there are not enough effective cards to make a tournament-level poison deck, but the Mosquito is the first step in that direction.

Blue

| Card Name: | ***Arcane Denial*** |
|---|---|
| **Casting Cost:** | 1U |
| **Card Type:** | Interrupt |
| **Card Text:** | Counter target spell. That spell's caster may draw up to two cards at the beginning of the next turn's upkeep. Draw a card at the beginning of the next turn's upkeep. |

**Arcane Denial Revealed:** Arcane Denial adds to blue's wide array of counter magic, with the drawback of a loss in card advantage. Countering a card with the Denial causes you to draw one card and the opponent to draw two, giving the opponent a 3/2 card advantage. Certain decks can overcome this disadvantage, however. In Millstone/Howling Mine decks the Denial's drawback is actually an advantage, speeding the process of exhausting an opponent's deck.

| Card Name: | ***Awesome Presence*** |
|---|---|
| **Casting Cost:** | U |
| **Card Type:** | Enchant Creature |
| **Card Text:** | Enchanted creature cannot be blocked unless defending player pays an additional 3 for each creature assigned to block enchanted creature. |

**Awesome Presence Revealed:** The Awesome Presence is weak. Although it is relatively cheap, it is unlikely to daunt an opponent past the first few turns. It could work well on an early Dervish when an opponent has little or no mana in play, but if the creature is removed with a Swords to Plowshares or a Lightning Bolt, the opponent enjoys a two-for-one card advantage. Do not expect to see this card used in any format.

| | |
|---|---|
| **Card Name:** | ***Benthic Explorers*** |
| **Casting Cost:** | 3U |
| **Card Type:** | Summon Merfolk (2/4) |
| **Card Text:** | T: Untap target tapped land an opponent controls to add one mana of any type that land produces to your mana pool. |

**Benthic Explorers Revealed:** The Benthic Explorers join the realm of the awesome and terrible Merfolk kingdom. And how awesome and terrible it is! Though I do not see them as functional cards, they can be another source of "fast" mana for blue. The effectiveness of this "fast" mana is questionable though. It will not help in the first few turns because the Explorers take such a long time to bring into play. Nonetheless, the Explorers are not bad creatures. A 2/4 for four mana is okay.

| | |
|---|---|
| **Card Name:** | ***Browse*** |
| **Casting Cost:** | 2UU |
| **Card Type:** | Enchantment |
| **Card Text:** | 2UU: Look at the top five cards of your library and put one of them into your |

hand. Remove the remaining four from the game.

**Browse Revealed:** When many players examine this card, they see its drawback and toss it into their junk cards. Actually, this card is similar in some ways to the Jayemdae Tome, and in many respects is better than the Tome. Consider that when you choose a card with Browse you get to look at five and pick one. That means if your deck ranks as even moderately good, you should receive a good card every time you pay Browse's activation cost. Another advantage of Browse is that you can activate it more than once a turn. Some players view Browse's ability as having to remove four cards each time you pay the activation cost. Think of the glass as half full, and you dig five cards down into your deck with each activation. Assuming you play it on the fourth turn in a sixty-card deck, you will be able to activate it eight times before running out of cards. Each of those cards will more than likely be the right card when you need it.

| | |
|---|---|
| **Card Name:** | *Diminishing Returns* |
| **Casting Cost:** | 2UU |
| **Card Type:** | Sorcery |
| **Card Text:** | Each player shuffles his or her hand and graveyard into his or her library. Remove the top ten cards from your library from the game. Each player draws up to seven cards. |

**Diminishing Returns Revealed:** This card will be abused. Its negative side effects are meaningless compared to the advantage it can give to its bearer. An obvious use of this card would be with a large number of Lightning Bolts, Incinerates, and direct damage. If you combine it with cheap cantrips like Lodestone Bauble, Barbed Sextant, and Urza's Bauble, it can provide its controller an unbelievable card advantage. You can drop many of these cards on the first turn and then use the Returns to refill your hand. Chances are that an opponent would not cast as many of his spells as the Diminishing Returns player. Also, when cast there is a high probability that its caster will draw another. Its penalty's only relevance is that it would be difficult to employ more than three in a sixty-card deck.

| | |
|---|---|
| **Card Name:** | *False Demise* |
| **Casting Cost:** | 2U |
| **Card Type:** | Enchant Creature |
| **Card Text:** | If enchanted creature is put into the graveyard, return that creature to play under your control as though it were just cast. |

**False Demise Revealed:** False Demise is an excellent creature enchantment. With the exception of having a creature removed from the game, the Demise allows you to maintain a creature in play regardless of what destruction is wrought on it. This card just begs for use with Jokulhaups. Imagine this situation: you cast an Orgg, followed with a False Demise. Next turn you cast Jokulhaups and destroy all land, creatures, and artifacts in play. Your Orgg returns to play at the end of the turn, and you smash your opponent in the course of a few rounds. This can also work well with Autumn Willow, if you are willing to use three colors. With Autumn Willow, it makes a tough creature even harder to kill.

| | |
|---|---|
| **Card Name:** | *Force of Will* |
| **Casting Cost:** | 3UU |
| **Card Type:** | Interrupt |
| **Card Text:** | You may pay 1 life and remove a blue card in your hand from the game instead of paying Force of Will's casting cost. Effects that prevent or redirect damage cannot be used to counter this loss of life. Counter target spell. |

**Force of Will Revealed:** Recently, a considerable amount of banter among many of the top players concerns the employment of Force of Will. A counter spell for its casting cost seems slightly expensive. But ponder that the Force allows players to take actions that they normally could not. If, for instance, you wish to cast something that will require you to tap out, you are not totally constrained by the lack of available mana. In a tight spot you can use the Force's "toss" ability as a last result. The toss ability has additional benefit in the early game, stopping nuisances like early Hymns. The Force also allows you to toss useless cards that are ineffective against certain decks (for instance a Control Magic when playing against a creatureless deck). Though the Force of Will is no Counterspell, I feel it fits well into many counter decks.

**Card Name:** *Foresight*

**Casting Cost:** 1U

**Card Type:** Sorcery

**Card Text:** Search your library for any three cards and remove them from the game. Shuffle your library afterwards. Draw a card at the beginning of the next turn's upkeep.

**Foresight Revealed:** This card adds a new twist to deck construction. With the Foresight, it is likely that more decks will run standard (not in the sideboard) color-specific cards. Foresight allows you to remove unnecessary cards while effectively increasing the probability of drawing a more useful card. For instance, if you have enough land in play for your deck to function throughout the rest of the game, you might use Foresight to remove excess land in the late game. In theory, you could play with one of each Circle of Protection, and Foresight out the unnecessary ones. Foresight is even more effective when used with cards like Brainstorm and Lat-Nam's Legacy. These cards allow you to place useless cards back in your library and then remove them when you draw the Foresight.

**Card Name:** *Lat-Nam's Legacy*

**Casting Cost:** 1U

**Card Type:** Instant

**Card Text:** Choose a card from your hand and shuffle that card into your library to draw two cards at the beginning of the next turn's upkeep.

**Lat-Nam's Legacy Revealed:** When a friend of mine showed me this card at the first Alliances sealed deck tournament he told me that it was almost as good as the Ancestral Recall. Upon closer inspection though, this card reveals that it is not anywhere near the level of the Ancestral Recall. When you take one card from your hand and return it to the deck, you are not trimming the deck out beyond a regular cantrip. Lat-Nam's Legacy is a waste of time.

| **Card Name:** | *Library of Lat-Nam* |
|---|---|
| **Casting Cost:** | 4U |
| **Card Type:** | Sorcery |
| **Card Text:** | Target opponent chooses one: you draw three cards at the beginning of the next turn's upkeep; or you search your library for a card, put it into your hand, and then shuffle your library. |

**Library of Lat-Nam Revealed:** This card is nice but self limiting. It is not really comparable to the Demonic Tutor or the Ancestral Recall because of its great expense. It is unquestionable that this is a good card, and that it will appear in a number of tournament level decks. One of the nicer elements of the Library is that it only requires one blue mana to cast. This means that it will fit in many decks where blue is a support color. High casting cost relegates the Library of Lat-Nam to a mid- to late-game card. There is a great deal of debate as to which effect of the Library is strongest. I believe that the answer depends on the situation. If your opponent casts a Library and you are at five life, have no counter spell, and you suspect he has a Fireball in his deck, it is obviously best to let him draw three cards. In many cases you should just let your opponent search for one card, especially if you hold a counter spell.

| | |
|---|---|
| **Card Name:** | ***Phantasmal Sphere*** |
| **Casting Cost:** | 1U |
| **Card Type:** | Summon Phantasm (0/1) |
| **Card Text:** | Flying. At the beginning of the upkeep, put a +1/+1 counter on Phantasmal Sphere. During your upkeep, pay 1 for each of these +1/+1 counters or bury Phantasmal Sphere. If Phantasmal Sphere leaves play, put an Orb token into play under your opponent's control. Treat this token as a */* blue creature with flying, where * is equal to the number of these +1/+1 counters on Phantasmal Sphere. |

**Phantasmal Sphere Revealed:** The Phantasmal Sphere is a very difficult creature to use effectively. If an opponent removes the creature (via Incinerate, Swords to Plowshares, Exile, etc.) he gets a creature and eliminates a creature for the cost of one card. This makes the Sphere difficult to employ. In sealed deck play where creature removal is less common, this card is much stronger. One strategy to negate the token creature is to use Unsummon or Word of Binding to remove it. This strategy still entails a card cost penalty. While the Sphere will eliminate an opponent in six turns if not removed, I still would not employ it in any of my tournament decks. The amount of removal in the Magic environment makes this card too dangerous to use.

| | |
|---|---|
| **Card Name:** | *Soldevi Heretic* |
| **Casting Cost:** | 2U |
| **Card Type:** | Summon Heretic (2/2) |
| **Card Text:** | W, T: Prevent up to 2 damage to any creature. Target opponent may draw a card. |

**Soldevi Heretic Revealed:** The Soldevi Heretic is a 2/2 creature with the same relative casting cost as a Gray Ogre. Its special ability is a double-edged sword. Giving an opponent cards is a hazard, although this hazard might turn to a benefit in a Howling Mine deck. One of the major problems I see with this creature is that it must tap to use its ability. That means that if you fear a Lightning Bolt, you must not commit the creature to an attack. Once again, this is not a creature I expect to see in any tournament-level deck.

| | |
|---|---|
| **Card Name:** | *Soldevi Sage* |
| **Casting Cost:** | 1U |
| **Card Type:** | Summon Wizard (1/1) |
| **Card Text:** | T: Sacrifice two lands to draw three cards. Choose and discard one of those cards. |

**Soldevi Sage Revealed:** The Soldevi Sage is a relatively strong creature in the right deck. Utilized with a large number of inexpensive cards, you could draw cards when excess land is in play without the threat of being unable to cast spells. You could use this card in combination with Reinforcements to rebuild a Wrathed army of creatures. The Soldevi Sage is also relatively cheap and can deal a fair amount of early damage. If an opponent destroys a land, you can use the Sage in response and draw an extra two cards at the cost of only one land. This creature also works well with Land Tax and Armageddon. When casting an Armageddon, you can tap out and sacrifice lands to draw cards.

| Card Name: | ***Spiny Starfish*** |
|---|---|
| **Casting Cost:** | 2U |
| **Card Type:** | Summon Starfish (0/1) |
| **Card Text:** | U: Regenerate. At the end of any turn in which Spiny Starfish is regenerated, put a Starfish token into play for each time it regenerated that turn. Treat these tokens as 0/1 blue creatures. |

**Spiny Starfish Revealed:** Sealed deck format best suits the Starfish, but you can create some uses for the Starfish in a constructed format. With a Sunken City, a wall of 0/1 blockers can become an army of 1/2s. Or, perhaps, combine the Spiny Starfish with Ashnod's Altar to produce a large amount of mana to fuel a game-winning Fireball. I am skeptical of the Starfish though, because it cannot deal damage without an enchantment, making it too defensive and one-dimensional for my taste.

| Card Name: | ***Storm Crow*** |
|---|---|
| **Casting Cost:** | 1U |
| **Card Type:** | Summon Bird (1/2) |
| **Card Text:** | Flying. |

**Storm Crow Revealed:** The Storm Crow is yet another addition to blue's flying hordes. Compared to the Bird Maiden it is a relatively good card, but I prefer Flying Men in Type I and Sea Sprites in Type II.

| Card Name: | ***Storm Elemental*** |
|---|---|
| **Casting Cost:** | 5U |
| **Card Type:** | Summon Elemental (3/4) |
| **Card Text:** | Flying. U: Remove the top card of your library from the game to tap target creature with flying. U: Remove the top card of your library from the game. If that card is a snow-covered land, Storm Elemental gets +1/+1 until end of turn. |

**Storm Elemental Revealed:** The Storm Elemental's expense outweighs its special ability; a 3/4 creature for six mana is no bargain. Using the Storm Elemental also requires the use of snow-covered lands, which increases the potency of Icequakes and Thermokarst. The Elemental is perhaps best employed in decks that use the Sylvan Library. This gives its caster the ability to not only boost the Elemental's power when necessary, but also allows him to cycle through his deck to find the right card at the right time.

**Card Name:** *Suffocation*

**Casting Cost:** 1U

**Card Type:** Instant

**Card Text:** Play only when a red sorcery or instant deals damage to you. Suffocation deals 4 damage to that spell's caster. Draw a card at the beginning of the next turn's upkeep.

**Suffocation Revealed:** Suffocation has a rather constrained range of use. It is nice in decks that contain a high degree of damage-dealing capacity, but most blue decks are passive. Because Suffocation is a cantrip, its use is not a total waste, but I do not believe it will fit well in many decks. It is a sideboard card.

**Card Name:** *Thought Lash*

**Casting Cost:** 2UU

**Card Type:** Enchantment

**Card Text:** Cumulative Upkeep: Remove the top card of your library from the game. If you do not, remove your library from the game and bury Thought Lash. 0: Remove the top card of your library from the game to prevent 1 damage to you.

**Thought Lash Revealed:** When I first saw this card I asked myself, "Why?" Was Wizards of the Coast attempting to make a worse card than Sorrow's Path? Or was it evidence of deeper emotional problems that could best be handled in therapy? There are some cards you can combine with the Lash to make it interesting, but it would require a player to build his deck around it. One possibility includes a Soldevi Digger and some direct damage. For instance, you cast a Lightning Bolt one turn, then play the Thought Lash. During your upkeep, you do not pay for the Lash and it removes the library. Then, use the Digger to put the Lightning Bolt on the bottom of the deck, making it the only card in the deck. You draw the Bolt, then Bolt your opponent, repeating the process until he dies.

| | |
|---|---|
| **Card Name:** | *Tidal Control* |
| **Casting Cost:** | 1UU |
| **Card Type:** | Enchantment |
| **Card Text:** | Cumulative Upkeep: 2. Any player may pay 2 or 2 life to counter target red or green spell. Play this ability as an interrupt. Effects that prevent or redirect damage cannot be used to counter this loss of life. |

**Tidal Control Revealed:** Tidal Control is blue's color specific card in the Alliances set and is the weakest of the five. This is a fair card but I would be reluctant to employ it. Its cumulative upkeep ensures that it will not remain in play for long, relegating it to the mid or late game. This card is also more of a stall card. It will not affect anything in hand or play.

| | |
|---|---|
| **Card Name:** | *Viscerid Armor* |
| **Casting Cost:** | 1U |
| **Card Type:** | Enchant Creature |
| **Card Text:** | Enchanted creature gets +1/+1. 1U: Return Viscerid Armor to owner's hand. |

**Viscerid Armor Revealed:** This card complements blue's card pool nicely. The Armor is a very durable creature enchantment. If an opponent tries to disenchant it, you can return it to your hand, or if he or she eliminates the creature it enchants, you may still return it to your hand and place it on another creature.

| | |
|---|---|
| **Card Name:** | *Viscerid Drone* |
| **Casting Cost:** | 1U |
| **Card Type:** | Summon Homarid (1/2) |
| **Card Text:** | T: Sacrifice a creature and a swamp to bury target non-artifact creature. T: Sacrifice a creature and a snow-covered swamp to bury target creature. |

**Viscerid Drone Revealed:** The Viscerid Drone is a good creature. Though little room remains for this creature in constructed deck environments, it would operate extremely efficiently in a sealed or draft environment. Its special ability is particularly strong in the late game, when there is a great deal of excess land in play. The Drone's optimum time of use would be during the fast effects phase immediately after declaration of blockers. A player can block with a creature, then sacrifice it to the Drone to eliminate an unblocked attacker.

# White

| | |
|---|---|
| **Card Name:** | *Carrier Pigeons* |
| **Casting Cost:** | 3W |
| **Card Type:** | Summon Pigeons (1/1) |
| **Card Text:** | Flying. Draw a card at the beginning of the upkeep of the turn after Carrier Pigeons comes into play. |

**Carrier Pigeons Revealed:** Carrier Pigeons has nothing to do with a constructed deck. It is a waste of time and too expensive for a small flying creature. Because of its casting cost, it is a midgame card, yet as a 1/1 flyer it is unlikely to impact the mid-game. This means the Carrier Pigeons absorbs a card slot, only delaying its caster from drawing a card that might help him significantly. If you wanted to trouble yourself, you could build a concept deck around the Pigeons with Enduring Renewal and Ashnod's Altar. By continually sacrificing the Carrier Pigeons to the Altar and recasting it with one white and one other, you could draw more cards. But like all combinations, this is very fragile and will not fit in a tournament-level deck. Though I would use this card in a sealed or draft environment, I would never employ it in a constructed deck.

| | |
|---|---|
| **Card Name:** | *Errand of Duty* |
| **Casting Cost:** | 1W |
| **Card Type:** | Instant |
| **Card Text:** | Put a Knight token into play. Treat this token as a 1/1 white creature with banding. |

**Errand of Duty Revealed:** The Errand of Duty is among the best cards that white obtained in the Alliances set. The strategic value of an instant 1/1 banding creature lies in the attack phase. For example, let's suppose that an opponent attacks with a Force of Nature, and you have an Erhnam, a Giant Spider, and a Dancing Scimitar in play. You can cast the Errand of Duty, band all of the creatures together killing the Force of Nature, and then distribute the damage (four points each) between the Dancing Scimitar and the Erhnam. Clearly, the Errand of Duty induces a new and exciting element of surprise defense to the game.

| | |
|---|---|
| **Card Name:** | *Exile* |
| **Casting Cost:** | 2W |
| **Card Type:** | Instant |
| **Card Text:** | Remove target non-white attacking creature from the game. Gain life equal to that creature's toughness. |

**Exile Revealed:** Exile is the best card that white received in the Alliances set. It gives white yet another method for gaining life and maintaining creature control. This card is much stronger as a sideboard card than as one in the regular deck. Against certain decks using a high degree of protection from white or white creatures it would serve no purpose.

| | |
|---|---|
| **Card Name:** | *Inheritance* |
| **Casting Cost:** | W |
| **Card Type:** | Enchantment |
| **Card Text:** | 3: Draw a card. Use this ability only when a creature is put into the graveyard from play and only once for each creature put into the graveyard. |

**Inheritance Revealed:** Inheritance is a strong card to add to a white creature deck. Unlike the Jayemdae Tome, you can activate it multiple times in a given turn, provided that you receive the opportunity and own enough mana. If an opponent casts a Wrath of God eliminating several creatures with one card, the holder of Inheritance will have the ability to recover the loss of card advantage.

| | |
|---|---|
| **Card Name:** | *Ivory Gargoyle* |
| **Casting Cost:** | 4W |
| **Card Type:** | Summon Gargoyle (2/2) |
| **Card Text:** | Flying. If Ivory Gargoyle is put into the graveyard from play, put it into play under owner's control at end of turn and skip your next draw phase. 4W: Remove Ivory Gargoyle from the game. |

**Ivory Gargoyle Revealed:** The Ivory Gargoyle is one of the unique creatures in the Alliances expansion. Its intriguing ability to return to play after going to the graveyard makes it very difficult to eliminate. The only means for an opponent to overcome a Gargoyle is to remove it from the game, counter it, or steal it. The Gargoyle's drawback is that you lose your next turn's draw phase if it goes to the graveyard. This is also cumulative, so if you have two in play and an opponent casts a Wrath of God, then you cannot draw a card for the next two turns. This drawback could create problems if an opponent has the advantage with cards in play and a Stormbind. If the Gargoyle becomes too much of a problem, you can remove it from the game yourself. The Gargoyle works well with mass destruction cards like Jokulhaups. You could cast a Haups after playing the Gargoyle, destroying everything except enchantments and your Gargoyle.

| | |
|---|---|
| **Card Name:** | ***Juniper Order Advocate*** |
| **Casting Cost:** | 2W |
| **Card Type:** | Summon Knight (1/2) |
| **Card Text:** | As long as Juniper Order Advocate is untapped, all green creatures you control get +1/+1. |

**Juniper Order Advocate Revealed:** The Juniper Order Advocate enhances the power and toughness of green creatures, although I believe that the Advocate is difficult to utilize. First, with only a two toughness it is very easy to remove. I do not see the Juniper Order Advocate as a very powerful addition to the constructed deck card pool, but it may assist in sealed or draft environments.

| Card Name: | ***Kjeldoran Escort*** |
|---|---|
| Casting Cost: | 2WW |
| Card Type: | Summon Soldier (2/3) |
| Card Text: | Banding. |

**Kjeldoran Escort Revealed:** The Kjeldoran Escort is an expensive and silly creature. Four mana is quite a bit to pay for a creature that can be removed with a Lightning Bolt or an Incinerate. When compared to a creature like the Benalish Hero, a 1/1 bander for one white mana, one can see that the Escort lacks economy.

| Card Name: | ***Kjeldoran Home Guard*** |
|---|---|
| Casting Cost: | 3W |
| Card Type: | Summon Soldier (1/6) |
| Card Text: | At the end of any combat in which Kjeldoran Home Guard attacked or blocked, put a -0/-1 counter on Kjeldoran Home Guard and put a Deserter token into play. Treat this token as a 0/1 white creature. |

**Kjeldoran Home Guard Revealed:** The Kjeldoran Home Guard constitutes a strong addition to white. Its ability to produce Deserter tokens can operate well with cards like Crusade or Ashnod's Altar and can also accompany a white weenie deck with a large number of banders. Its six toughness allows it to absorb a fair amount of damage while creating Deserter tokens, which can then suck up any damage dealt by attackers when the band blocks. The Home Guard is a stronger creature in a constructed

environment where cards that can support it, like
Crusade, are widely available, as opposed to the limitations of a sealed deck environment.

| Card Name: | **_Kjeldoran Pride_** |
|---|---|
| **Casting Cost:** | 1W |
| **Card Type:** | Enchant Creature |
| **Card Text:** | Enchanted creature gets +1/+2. 2U: Switch Kjeldoran Pride from creature it enchants to another creature. Kjeldoran Pride's new target must be legal. Treat Kjeldoran Pride as though it were just cast on the new target. |

**Kjeldoran Pride Revealed.** The Kjeldoran Pride is
another creature enchantment that is less likely to be
removed. The confining element of the Pride is that it
requires its controller to use blue for him to enjoy its
maximum benefits. Even though you can avoid losing
the Pride to Swords to Plowshares, Lightning Bolt, or
Terror if you have another creature in play, it will still
vanish with a Wrath of God, Jokulhaups, or Nevinyrral's
Disk. This card is very strong in sealed or draft
environments but suffers in a constructed deck
environment.

| Card Name: | *Martyrdom* |
|---|---|
| **Casting Cost:** | 1WW |
| **Card Type:** | Instant |
| **Card Text:** | Until end of turn, you may redirect to target creature you control any amount of damage. |

**Martyrdom Revealed:** Martyrdom seems to mimic a Simulacrum at first glance, but on closer inspection you will notice that the damage does not need to be directed at the caster. An opponent could cast a Pyroclasym, and you could redirect all of that damage to a single creature, preserving the remaining creatures in play. This is not merely a sideboard card either, as most decks you face focus on dealing some form of damage. However, Martyrdom may not work against decks that achieve victory by running opponents out of cards. Martyrdom operates well in both sealed and constructed environments.

| Card Name: | *Noble Steeds* |
|---|---|
| **Casting Cost:** | 2W |
| **Card Type:** | Enchantment |
| **Card Text:** | 1W: Target creature gains first strike until end of turn. |

**Noble Steeds Revealed:** Noble Steeds aids in most decks with a creature theme. Though this card is only useful against other decks with creatures of their own, the Steeds could provide the edge in combat needed to overcome a foe. I have seen the Steeds used in an Ice Age/Alliances deck with Elvish Rangers, and it made the

Ranger quite a formidable creature. Though I do not foresee this card surfacing in constructed deck, it will be a strong asset for any sealed or draft deck that contains a large amount of white.

| | |
|---|---|
| **Card Name:** | *Reinforcements* |
| **Casting Cost:** | W |
| **Card Type:** | Instant |
| **Card Text:** | Put up to three target creature cards from you graveyard on top of your library in any order. |

**Reinforcements Revealed:** Reinforcements furnishes a creature deck player the ability to recuperate from mass creature destruction. When used with cards like Inheritance or the Soldevi Sage, a player can quickly recover his creatures. Reinforcements is a strong card in constructed environments and even stronger in a sealed or draft environment.

| | |
|---|---|
| **Card Name:** | *Reprisal* |
| **Casting Cost:** | 1W |
| **Card Type:** | Instant |
| **Card Text:** | Bury target creature with power 4 or greater. |

**Reprisal Revealed:** Reprisal affords white a strong sideboard card. It helps eliminate cards such as Erhnams,

Serra Angels, Vampires, and Lhurgoyfs. Used with Wrath of God, Swords to Plowshares, and Exile, white becomes nearly impervious to creatures without protection from white. I would not use Reprisal in a standard deck, but I would certainly consider it for the sideboard.

| | |
|---|---|
| **Card Name:** | *Royal Decree* |
| **Casting Cost:** | 2WW |
| **Card Type:** | Enchantment |
| **Card Text:** | Cumulative Upkeep: W. Whenever a swamp, mountain, black permanent, or red permanent becomes tapped, Royal Decree deals 1 damage to that permanent's controller. |

**Royal Decree Revealed:** Royal Decree is white's color-specific card from Alliances. This card stalls a red or black player, but it fails to measure to the power of its black counterpart Dystopia. One of the nice features of each of the multi-color basher cards in Alliances is that they cover more decks and occupy less space in the sideboard.

| | |
|---|---|
| **Card Name:** | *Royal Herbalist* |
| **Casting Cost:** | W |
| **Card Type:** | Summon Cleric (1/1) |
| **Card Text:** | 2: Remove the top card of your library from the game to gain 1 life. |

**Royal Herbalist Revealed:** The Royal Herbalist is a solid card. First, it's a 1/1 creature for one mana with a decent special ability. In a tight spot it could very easily save its controller from termination. In addition, like the Chaos Harlequin, it can attend Sylvan Library to cycle through different cards to find the ones you need. Although the Herbalist is a stronger card in the sealed and draft environments, it might show up in a few tournament-level constructed decks.

| | |
|---|---|
| **Card Name:** | *Scars of the Veteran* |
| **Casting Cost:** | 4W |
| **Card Type:** | Instant |
| **Card Text:** | You may remove a white card in your hand from the game instead of paying Scars of the Veteran's casting cost. Prevent up to 7 damage to target creature or player. For each 1 damage to a creature prevented by Scars of the Veteran put a +0/+1 counter on that creature at end of turn. |

**Scars of the Veteran Revealed:** Scars of the Veteran is white's "toss" card. It performs well with creatures, and particularly well on a creature with protection from white. You can do this because cards like Scars of the Veteran and Healing Salve target the damage and not the creature. If you use it on a Black Knight just struck with a Lighting Bolt, you would receive a 2/5 Knight: a much more difficult creature to eliminate. The Scars is not really comparable in usefulness to Force of Will, but it may still find its place in the Magic environment. I do not believe that this card fits into many tournament-level constructed decks, but it would make a worthy selection in any sealed or draft environment.

| | |
|---|---|
| **Card Name:** | *Seasoned Tactician* |
| **Casting Cost:** | 2W |
| **Card Type:** | Summon Tactician (1/3) |
| **Card Text:** | 3: Remove the top four cards of your library from the game to prevent all damage to you from one source. |

**Seasoned Tactician Revealed:** The Seasoned Tactician's aptitude suits sealed and draft environments. In a sealed or draft environment, an opponent must eliminate the Tactician before eliminating you. In many cases, this bestows the Tactician's controller the time necessary to recover and eventually gain control of the game. If the source of damage is permanent, the Tactician is much less useful. Eventually, its controller will run out of cards (more likely in a sealed or draft environment because most players only use a forty-card deck). In constructed deck environments the Tactician is easily removed and ineffective.

| | |
|---|---|
| **Card Name:** | *Sustaining Spirit* |
| **Casting Cost:** | 1W |
| **Card Type:** | Summon Guardian (0/3) |

**Card Text:** Cumulative Upkeep: 1W. Any damage that would reduce your life total to less than 1 instead reduces it to 1.

**Sustaining Spirit Revealed:** The Sustaining Spirit resembles the Ali from Cairo. Like the Tactician, this card is much more useful in a sealed or draft environment where it is less likely to be removed. In constructed deck, this creature will disappear as soon as it becomes a nuisance.

**Card Name:** *Sworn Defender*

**Casting Cost:** 2WW

**Card Type:** Summon Knight (1/3)

**Card Text:** 1: Change Sworn Defender's power to the toughness of target creature blocking or being blocked by Sworn Defender, minus 1, until end of turn. Change Sworn Defender's toughness to 1 plus the power of that creature, until end of turn.

**Sworn Defender Revealed:** The Sworn Defender is an excellent sealed or draft deck creature and a marginal constructed deck creature. If you place a card like Armor of Faith or Holy Strength on the Sworn Defender, you receive a creature that will eliminate any opposing creature in combat by using its special ability. The Defender can also aid decks with banders. With the Defender, you can band and then assign any damage dealt in combat to the Defender, while the other banding creature can provide the extra point of damage to eliminate an opposing blocker or attacker.

| Card Name: | ***Unlikely Alliance*** |
|---|---|
| Casting Cost: | 1W |
| Card Type: | Enchantment |
| Card Text: | 1W: Target non-attacking, non-blocking creature gets +0/+2 until end of turn. |

**Unlikely Alliance Revealed:** This card protects your creatures from other creatures and direct damage. Though you cannot use this ability during the attack phase, you can use it before. For example, if you declare an attack with an Erhnam Djinn and I have a Benalish Hero in play, I can respond to your declaration by using the Unlikely Alliance twice to boost the Hero to a 1/5 and block the Erhnam. This card operates efficiently in sealed and constructed environments. If an opponent casts a Pyroclasym, you can save a creature for each two mana you have in play. The Alliance assists Mishra's Factories as well, which becomes a great asset when you fear the possibility of a Lightning Bolt. Also the Alliance is an excellent card to add to any deck with a large number of banders. You can easily distribute damage dealt by blocking creatures to a creature targeted by the Unlikely Alliance earlier in the turn.

| Card Name: | ***Wild Aesthir*** |
|---|---|
| Casting Cost: | 2W |
| Card Type: | Summon Aesthir (1/1) |
| Card Text: | Flying, first strike. WW: +2/+0 until end of turn. You cannot spend more than WW in this way each turn. |

**Wild Aesthir Revealed:** The Wild Aesthir gives white a cheap flying creature that can deal a relatively large amount of damage. This creature is even better than its Legends counterpart, Thunder Spirit, in the respect that it can deal a greater amount of damage, although the Thunder Spirit is less susceptible to Serrated Arrows and requires no mana to pump. In the late game, though, with a couple of Crusades, the Aesthir's value skyrockets. The Aesthir plays well in both the sealed/draft and constructed deck environments.

# *Decks*

This section contains a collection of sixteen tournament-level decks. The first three are the Nationals decks from the 1996 National Championship. Both mine (finalist) and Denis Bently's (National Champion) are exact reproductions. The Stasis deck is representative of both Mike Long's (semi-finalist) and Matt Place's (semi-finalist) decks. This is because they collaborated on the design of their decks and they were virtually identical. The next seven decks are different Type II tournament decks that contain Alliances cards. The final six decks are Ice Age/Alliances decks. Each of the sixteen decks are excellent to test new decks against.

# Denis Bentley's Necro Deck

| Block 1 | Block 2 | Block 3 |
|---------|---------|---------|
| **Pocket 1** | **Pocket 1** | **Pocket 1** |
| Hymn to Tourach | Black Vise | Strip Mine |
| Hymn to Tourach | Dystopia | Strip Mine |
| Hymn to Tourach | Ivory Tower | Sulfurous Springs |
| Hymn to Tourach | Zuran Orb | Sulfurous Springs |
| **Pocket 2** | **Pocket 2** | **Pocket 2** |
| Dark Ritual | Necropotence | Sulfurous Springs |
| Dark Ritual | Necropotence | Sulfurous Springs |
| Dark Ritual | Necropotence | Swamp |
| Dark Ritual | Fireball | Swamp |
| **Pocket 3** | **Pocket 3** | **Pocket 3** |
| Hypnotic Specter | Icequake | Swamp |
| Hypnotic Specter | Icequake | Swamp |
| Hypnotic Specter | Icequake | Swamp |
| Hypnotic Specter | Icequake | Swamp |
| **Pocket 4** | **Pocket 4** | **Pocket 4** |
| Order of the Ebon Hand | Lightning Bolt | Swamp |
| Order of the Ebon Hand | Lightning Bolt | Swamp |
| Order of the Ebon Hand | Lightning Bolt | Swamp |
| Order of the Ebon Hand | Lightning Bolt | Swamp |
| **Pocket 5** | **Pocket 5** | **Pocket 5** |
| Black Knight | City of Brass | Swamp |
| Black Knight | City of Brass | Swamp |
| Black Knight | Strip Mine | Swamp |
| Black Knight | Strip Mine | Swamp |

**Sideboard**

1. Dystopia
2. Dystopia
3. Dystopia
4. Jester's Cap
5. Shatter
6. Serrated Arrows
7. Serrated Arrows
8. Dance of the Dead
9. Dance of the Dead
10. Contagion
11. Infernal Darkness
12. Stromgald Kabald
13. Stromgald Kabald
14. Dark Banishing
15. Dark Banishing

## The Turbo Stasis Deck

| Block 1 | Block 2 | Block 3 |
|---|---|---|
| **Pocket 1** | **Pocket 1** | **Pocket 1** |
| Force of Will | Howling Mine | Adarkar Wastes |
| Force of Will | Howling Mine | Adarkar Wastes |
| Force of Will | Howling Mine | Adarkar Wastes |
| Force of Will | Howling Mine | Adarkar Wastes |
| **Pocket 2** | **Pocket 2** | **Pocket 2** |
| Arcane Denial | Despotic Scepter | City of Brass |
| Arcane Denial | Despotic Scepter | City of Brass |
| Arcane Denial | Despotic Scepter | Island |
| Arcane Denial | Ivory Tower | Island |
| **Pocket 3** | **Pocket 3** | **Pocket 3** |
| Stasis | Kismet | Island |
| Stasis | Kismet | Island |
| Stasis | Kismet | Island |
| Stasis | Zuran Orb | Island |
| **Pocket 4** | **Pocket 4** | **Pocket 4** |
| Boomerang | Recall | Island |
| Boomerang | Recall | Island |
| Boomerang | Land Tax | Island |
| Boomerang | Feldon's Cane | Island |
| **Pocket 5** | **Pocket 5** | **Pocket 5** |
| Lim-Dûl's Vault | Underground River | Island |
| Lim-Dûl's Vault | Underground River | Island |
| Lim-Dûl's Vault | Underground River | Island |
| Lim-Dûl's Vault | Underground River | Island |

**Sideboard**

1. Disenchant
2. Disenchant
3. Swords to Plowshares
4. Swords to Plowshares
5. Black Vise
6. Wall of Air
7. Wall of Air
8. Power Sink
9. Power Sink
10. Blue Elemental Blast
11. Blue Elemental Blast
12. Blue Elemental Blast
13. Feldon's Cane
14. Tormod's Crypt
15. Mana Short

# *My Song Deck*

| Block 1 | Block 2 | Block 3 |
|---|---|---|
| **Pocket 1** | **Pocket 1** | **Pocket 1** |
| Serrated Arrows | Aeolipile | Strip Mine |
| Serrated Arrows | Aeolipile | Strip Mine |
| Serrated Arrows | Aeolipile | Strip Mine |
| Serrated Arrows | Divine Offering | Strip Mine |
| **Pocket 2** | **Pocket 2** | **Pocket 2** |
| Icy Manipulator | Divine Offering | Brushland |
| Icy Manipulator | Disenchant | Brushland |
| Icy Manipulator | Disenchant | Brushland |
| Icy Manipulator | Disenchant | Brushland |
| **Pocket 3** | **Pocket 3** | **Pocket 3** |
| Winter Orb | Swords to Plowshares | Adarkar Wastes |
| Winter Orb | Swords to Plowshares | Adarkar Wastes |
| Winter Orb | Swords to Plowshares | Adarkar Wastes |
| Deadly Insects | Swords to Plowshares | Plains |
| **Pocket 4** | **Pocket 4** | **Pocket 4** |
| Black Vise | Wrath of God | Mishra's Factory |
| Land Tax | Wrath of God | Mishra's Factory |
| Sylvan Library | Fellwar Stone | Mishra's Factory |
| Balance | Fellwar Stone | Plains |
| **Pocket 5** | **Pocket 5** | **Pocket 5** |
| Titania's Song | Fellwar Stone | Plains |
| Titania's Song | Fellwar Stone | Plains |
| Armageddon | Forest | Plains |
| Armageddon | City of Brass | Plains |
| | | Plains |

**Sideboard**

1. Adarkar Wastes
2. Blue Elemental Blast
3. Blue Elemental Blast
4. Blue Elemental Blast
5. Slight of Mind
6. Wrath of God
7. Serra Angel
8. Serra Angel
9. Serra Angel
10. Disenchant
11. Slight of Mind
12. Disrupting Scepter
13. Winter Orb
14. Zuran Orb
15. Ivory Tower

# *Criss Prat's Hunka Do*

| Block 1 | Block 2 | Block 3 |
|---|---|---|
| **Pocket 1** | **Pocket 1** | **Pocket 1** |
| Howling Mine | Wrath of God | Strip Mine |
| Howling Mine | Wrath of God | Strip Mine |
| Howling Mine | Zuran Orb | Strip Mine |
| Howling Mine | Ivory Tower | Strip Mine |
| **Pocket 2** | **Pocket 2** | **Pocket 2** |
| Winter Orb | Icy Manipulator | Adarkar Wastes |
| Winter Orb | Icy Manipulator | Adarkar Wastes |
| Winter Orb | Icy Manipulator | Adarkar Wastes |
| Winter Orb | Icy Manipulator | Adarkar Wastes |
| **Pocket 3** | **Pocket 3** | **Pocket 3** |
| Armageddon | Swords to Plowshares | Mountain |
| Balance | Swords to Plowshares | Mountain |
| Recall | Swords to Plowshares | Mountain |
| Recall | Swords to Plowshares | Mountain |
| **Pocket 4** | **Pocket 4** | **Pocket 4** |
| Pyroclasm | Disenchant | Mountain |
| Pyroclasm | Disenchant | Mountain |
| Pyroclasm | Disenchant | Mountain |
| Pyroclasm | Primitive Justice | Plains |
| **Pocket 5** | **Pocket 5** | **Pocket 5** |
| Tormod's Crypt | Fellwar Stone | Plains |
| Feldon's Cane | Fellwar Stone | Plains |
| Serrated Arrows | City of Brass | Plains |
| Serrated Arrows | City of Brass | Plains |

**Sideboard**
1. Red Elemental Blast
2. Red Elemental Blast
3. Red Elemental Blast
4. Millstone
5. Millstone
6. Tormod's Crypt
7. Feldon's Cane
8. Primitive Justice
9. Mana Short
10. Mana Short
11. Serrated Arrows
12. Divine Offering
13. Arcane Denial
14. Arcane Denial
15. Arcane Denial

# *Alliance's Modified Necro*

| Block 1 | Block 2 | Block 3 |
|---|---|---|
| **Pocket 1** | **Pocket 1** | **Pocket 1** |
| Order of the Ebon Hand | Hymn to Tourach | Strip Mine |
| Order of the Ebon Hand | Hymn to Tourach | Strip Mine |
| Order of the Ebon Hand | Hymn to Tourach | Swamp |
| Order of the Ebon Hand | Hymn to Tourach | Swamp |
| **Pocket 2** | **Pocket 2** | **Pocket 2** |
| Knights of Stromgald | Drain Life | Swamp |
| Knights of Stromgald | Drain Life | Swamp |
| Phantasmal Fiend | Drain Life | Swamp |
| Phantasmal Fiend | Contagion | Swamp |
| **Pocket 3** | **Pocket 3** | **Pocket 3** |
| Hypnotic Specter | Dark Ritual | Swamp |
| Hypnotic Specter | Dark Ritual | Swamp |
| Hypnotic Specter | Dark Ritual | Swamp |
| Hypnotic Specter | Dark Ritual | Swamp |
| **Pocket 4** | **Pocket 4** | **Pocket 4** |
| Nevinyrral's Disk | Demonic Consultation | Swamp |
| Nevinyrral's Disk | Demonic Consultation | Swamp |
| Nevinyrral's Disk | Contagion | Swamp |
| Nevinyrral's Disk | Mishra's Factory | Swamp |
| **Pocket 5** | **Pocket 5** | **Pocket 5** |
| Necropotence | Mishra's Factory | Swamp |
| Necropotence | Mishra's Factory | Swamp |
| Necropotence | Strip Mine | Swamp |
| Zuran Orb | Strip Mine | Swamp |

**Sideboard**

1. Contagion
2. Contagion
3. Terror
4. Terror
5. Dystopia
6. Dystopia
7. Dystopia
8. Dystopia
9. Serrated Arrows
10. Serrated Arrows
11. Serrated Arrows
12. Meekstone
13. Meekstone
14. Ivory Tower
15. Drain Life

# The Outpost Disk Deck

| Block 1 | Block 2 | Block 3 |
|---|---|---|
| **Pocket 1** | **Pocket 1** | **Pocket 1** |
| Nevinyrral's Disk | Power Sink | City of Brass |
| Nevinyrral's Disk | Zur's Weirding | City of Brass |
| Nevinyrral's Disk | Recall | Adarkar Wastes |
| Nevinyrral's Disk | Recall | Adarkar Wastes |
| **Pocket 2** | **Pocket 2** | **Pocket 2** |
| Kjeldoran Outpost | Lightning Bolt | Plains |
| Kjeldoran Outpost | Lightning Bolt | Plains |
| Kjeldoran Outpost | Lightning Bolt | Plains |
| Fireball | Lightning Bolt | Plains |
| **Pocket 3** | **Pocket 3** | **Pocket 3** |
| Thawing Glaciers | Incinerate | Plains |
| Thawing Glaciers | Incinerate | Plains |
| Thawing Glaciers | Fireball | Plains |
| Land Tax | Fireball | Plains |
| **Pocket 4** | **Pocket 4** | **Pocket 4** |
| Balance | Blinking Spirit | Plains |
| Disenchant | Blinking Spirit | Mountain |
| Disenchant | Blinking Spirit | Mountain |
| Disenchant | City of Brass | Mountain |
| **Pocket 5** | **Pocket 5** | **Pocket 5** |
| Swords to Plowshares | Mishra's Factory | Mountain |
| Swords to Plowshares | Mishra's Factory | Mountain |
| Swords to Plowshares | Mishra's Factory | Mountain |
| Swords to Plowshares | Mishra's Factory | Mountain |

**Sideboard**

1. Disenchant
2. Primitive Justice
3. Primitive Justice
4. Reverse Damage
5. Reverse Damage
6. Reverse Damage
7. Power Sink
8. Pyroblast
9. Pyroblast
10. Exile
11. Exile
12. Exile
13. Exile
14. Disrupting Scepter
15. Disrupting Scepter

**115**

## The Weird Browse Deck

| Block 1 | Block 2 | Block 3 |
|---|---|---|
| **Pocket 1** | **Pocket 1** | **Pocket 1** |
| Browse | Zur's Weirding | City of Brass |
| Browse | Zur's Weirding | City of Brass |
| Browse | Zuran Orb | Adarkar Wastes |
| Browse | Ivory Tower | Adarkar Wastes |
| **Pocket 2** | **Pocket 2** | **Pocket 2** |
| Soldevi Digger | Control Magic | Adarkar Wastes |
| Soldevi Digger | Control Magic | Adarkar Wastes |
| Recall | Control Magic | Island |
| Recall | Force of Will | Island |
| **Pocket 3** | **Pocket 3** | **Pocket 3** |
| Lightning Bolt | Force of Will | Island |
| Lightning Bolt | Force of Will | Island |
| Lightning Bolt | Counterspell | Island |
| Lightning Bolt | Counterspell | Island |
| **Pocket 4** | **Pocket 4** | **Pocket 4** |
| Incinerate | Counterspell | Island |
| Incinerate | Counterspell | Island |
| Incinerate | Fireball | Mountain |
| Fireball | Fireball | Mountain |
| **Pocket 5** | **Pocket 5** | **Pocket 5** |
| Balance | Mishra's Factory | Mountain |
| Disenchant | Mishra's Factory | Mountain |
| Disenchant | Mishra's Factory | Mountain |
| Disenchant | City of Brass | Mountain |

**Sideboard**

| | | |
|---|---|---|
| 1. Pyroblast | 6. Hydroblast | 11. Land Tax |
| 2. Pyroblast | 7. Hydroblast | 12. Strip Mine |
| 3. Pyroblast | 8. Hydroblast | 13. Strip Mine |
| 4. Swords to Plowshares | 9. Control Magic | 14. Strip Mine |
| 5. Swords to Plowshares | 10. Disenchant | 15. Strip Mine |

# The Haups/Gargoyle Deck

| Block 1 | Block 2 | Block 3 |
|---|---|---|
| Pocket 1 | Pocket 1 | Pocket 1 |
| Mana Vault | Savannah Lion | City of Brass |
| Mana Vault | Savannah Lion | City of Brass |
| Mana Vault | Savannah Lion | Plains |
| Mana Vault | Savannah Lion | Plains |
| Pocket 2 | Pocket 2 | Pocket 2 |
| Manabarbs | Lightning Bolt | Ruins of Trokair |
| Manabarbs | Lightning Bolt | Ruins of Trokair |
| Manabarbs | Lightning Bolt | Ruins of Trokair |
| Zuran Orb | Lightning Bolt | Ruins of Trokair |
| Pocket 3 | Pocket 3 | Pocket 3 |
| Jokulhaups | Incinerate | Dwarven Ruins |
| Jokulhaups | Incinerate | Dwarven Ruins |
| Jokulhaups | Swords to Plowshares | Dwarven Ruins |
| Jokulhaups | Swords to Plowshares | Dwarven Ruins |
| Pocket 4 | Pocket 4 | Pocket 4 |
| Ivory Gargoyle | Disenchant | Mountain |
| Ivory Gargoyle | Disenchant | Mountain |
| Balance | Divine Offering | Mountain |
| Primitive Justice | Land Tax | Mountain |
| Pocket 5 | Pocket 5 | Pocket 5 |
| Ivory Tower | Mishra's Factory | Plains |
| Orgg | Mishra's Factory | Plains |
| Orgg | Mishra's Factory | Mountain |
| Black Vise | Mishra's Factory | Mountain |

**Sideboard**

1. Divine Offering
2. Divine Offering
3. Disenchant
4. Disenchant
5. Primitive Justice
6. Serrated Arrows
7. Serrated Arrows
8. Serrated Arrows
9. C.O.P. Red
10. C.O.P. Red
11. C.O.P. Red
12. Red Elemental Blast
13. Red Elemental Blast
14. Red Elemental Blast
15. Swords to Plowshares

# Creature, Creature, Creature, Creature...Stop That

| Block 1 | Block 2 | Block 3 |
|---|---|---|
| **Pocket 1** | **Pocket 1** | **Pocket 1** |
| Yavimaya Ants | Whirling Dervish | Mishra's Factory |
| Yavimaya Ants | Whirling Dervish | Mishra's Factory |
| Yavimaya Ants | Whirling Dervish | Mishra's Factory |
| Thelonite Druid | Whirling Dervish | Mishra's Factory |
| **Pocket 2** | **Pocket 2** | **Pocket 2** |
| Kaysa | Ernham Djinn | Forest |
| Kaysa | Ernham Djinn | Forest |
| Kaysa | Ernham Djinn | Forest |
| Force of Nature | Ernham Djinn | Forest |
| **Pocket 3** | **Pocket 3** | **Pocket 3** |
| Elvish Archers | Scavenger Folk | Forest |
| Elvish Archers | Scavenger Folk | Forest |
| Elvish Archers | Scavenger Folk | Forest |
| Elvish Archers | Scavenger Folk | Forest |
| **Pocket 4** | **Pocket 4** | **Pocket 4** |
| Llanowar Elves | Crumble | Forest |
| Llanowar Elves | Crumble | Forest |
| Llanowar Elves | Lhurgoyf | Forest |
| Llanowar Elves | Lhurgoyf | Forest |
| **Pocket 5** | **Pocket 5** | **Pocket 5** |
| Fyndhorn Elves | Lhurgoyf | Forest |
| Fyndhorn Elves | Deadly Insects | Forest |
| Fyndhorn Elves | Deadly Insects | Forest |
| Fyndhorn Elves | Forest | Forest |

## Sideboard

1. Tranquility
2. Tranquility
3. Tranquility
4. Tranquility
5. Essence Filter
6. Essence Filter
7. Crumble
8. Crumble
9. Nevinyrral's Disk
10. Nevinyrral's Disk
11. Nevinyrral's Disk
12. Disrupting Scepter
13. Disrupting Scepter
14. Disrupting Scepter
15. Disrupting Scepter

# The Too Many Bolts Deck

| Block 1 | Block 2 | Block 3 |
|---------|---------|---------|
| **Pocket 1** | **Pocket 1** | **Pocket 1** |
| Diminishing Returns | Nevinyrral's Disk | City of Brass |
| Diminishing Returns | Nevinyrral's Disk | City of Brass |
| Diminishing Returns | Nevinyrral's Disk | City of Brass |
| Diminishing Returns | Nevinyrral's Disk | Island |
| **Pocket 2** | **Pocket 2** | **Pocket 2** |
| Lightning Bolt | Force of Will | Island |
| Lightning Bolt | Force of Will | Island |
| Lightning Bolt | Force of Will | Island |
| Lightning Bolt | Recall | Island |
| **Pocket 3** | **Pocket 3** | **Pocket 3** |
| Incinerate | Power Sink | Island |
| Incinerate | Power Sink | Island |
| Incinerate | Power Sink | Island |
| Incinerate | Recall | Island |
| **Pocket 4** | **Pocket 4** | **Pocket 4** |
| Guerrilla Tactics | Jeweled Amulet | Mountain |
| Guerrilla Tactics | Jeweled Amulet | Mountain |
| Guerrilla Tactics | Jeweled Amulet | Mountain |
| Guerrilla Tactics | Jeweled Amulet | Mountain |
| **Pocket 5** | **Pocket 5** | **Pocket 5** |
| Fireball | Mishra's Factory | Mountain |
| Fireball | Mishra's Factory | Mountain |
| Fireball | Mishra's Factory | Mountain |
| Fireball | Mishra's Factory | Mountain |

**Sideboard**

| | | |
|---|---|---|
| 1. Pyroblast | 6. Hydroblast | 11. Control Magic |
| 2. Pyroblast | 7. Primitive Justice | 12. Control Magic |
| 3. Pyroblast | 8. Primitive Justice | 13. Anarchy |
| 4. Pyroblast | 9. Primitive Justice | 14. Anarchy |
| 5. Hydroblast | 10. Control Magic | 15. Anarchy |

# The Four-Color Haups Deck

| Block 1 | Block 2 | Block 3 |
|---|---|---|
| **Pocket 1** | **Pocket 1** | **Pocket 1** |
| Ivory Gargoyle | Lava Burst | Plains |
| Ivory Gargoyle | Lava Burst | Plains |
| Ivory Gargoyle | Lava Burst | Plains |
| Zuran Orb | Mind Warp | Plains |
| **Pocket 2** | **Pocket 2** | **Pocket 2** |
| Order of the White Shield | Power Sink | Swamp |
| Order of the White Shield | Power Sink | Sulfurous Springs |
| Blinking Spirit | Power Sink | Sulfurous Springs |
| Blinking Spirit | Pillage | Island |
| **Pocket 3** | **Pocket 3** | **Pocket 3** |
| Blinking Spirit | Pillage | Adarkar Wastes |
| Jokulhaups | Pillage | Adarkar Wastes |
| Jokulhaups | Disenchant | Adarkar Wastes |
| Jokulhaups | Thawing Glaciers | Adarkar Wastes |
| **Pocket 4** | **Pocket 4** | **Pocket 4** |
| Swords to Plowshares | Thawing Glaciers | Mountain |
| Swords to Plowshares | Thawing Glaciers | Mountain |
| Swords to Plowshares | Kjeldoran Outpost | Mountain |
| Swords to Plowshares | Kjeldoran Outpost | Mountain |
| **Pocket 5** | **Pocket 5** | **Pocket 5** |
| Incinerate | Plains | Mountain |
| Incinerate | Plains | Mountain |
| Incinerate | Plains | Mountain |
| Incinerate | Plains | Mountain |

**Sideboard**

| | | |
|---|---|---|
| 1. Pyroblast | 6. Exile | 11. Primitive Justice |
| 2. Pyroblast | 7. Exile | 12. Disenchant |
| 3. Pyroblast | 8. C.O.P. Green | 13. Disenchant |
| 4. Pyroblast | 9. C.O.P. Green | 14. Disenchant |
| 5. Kjeldoran Outpost | 10. Primitive Justice | 15. C.O.P. White |

# *Arachnophobia*

| Block 1 | Block 2 | Block 3 |
|---|---|---|
| **Pocket 1** | **Pocket 1** | **Pocket 1** |
| Trapdoor Spider | Yavimaya Ancients | Sulfurous Springs |
| Trapdoor Spider | Yavimaya Ancients | Sulfurous Springs |
| Trapdoor Spider | Orcish Cannoneers | Karplusan Forest |
| Trapdoor Spider | Orcish Cannoneers | Karplusan Forest |
| **Pocket 2** | **Pocket 2** | **Pocket 2** |
| Woolly Spider | Jokulhaups | Karplusan Forest |
| Woolly Spider | Jokulhaups | Karplusan Forest |
| Woolly Spider | Stormbind | Mountain |
| Woolly Spider | Giant Growth | Mountain |
| **Pocket 3** | **Pocket 3** | **Pocket 3** |
| Yavimya Ants | Incinerate | Mountain |
| Yavimya Ants | Incinerate | Mountain |
| Yavimya Ants | Incinerate | Forest |
| Yavimya Ants | Incinerate | Forest |
| **Pocket 4** | **Pocket 4** | **Pocket 4** |
| Fyndhorn Elves | Thawing Glaciers | Forest |
| Fyndhorn Elves | Thawing Glaciers | Forest |
| Fyndhorn Elves | Thawing Glaciers | Forest |
| Fyndhorn Elves | Mind Warp | Forest |
| **Pocket 5** | **Pocket 5** | **Pocket 5** |
| Orcish Lumberjack | Lava Burst | Forest |
| Orcish Lumberjack | Lava Burst | Forest |
| Orcish Lumberjack | Swamp | Forest |
| Orcish Lumberjack | Swamp | Forest |

**Sideboard**

1. Stormbind
2. Essence Filter
3. Essence Filter
4. Primitive Justice
5. Primitive Justice
6. Pyroblast
7. Pyroblast
8. Pyroblast
9. Pyroblast
10. Jokulhaups
11. Anarchy
12. Anarchy
13. Pillage
14. Pillage
15. Pillage

**121**

# Scott Martin's Horror Deck

| Block 1 | Block 2 | Block 3 |
|---|---|---|
| **Pocket 1** | **Pocket 1** | **Pocket 1** |
| Krovikan Horror | Kjeldoran Outpost | Plains |
| Krovikan Horror | Kjeldoran Outpost | Plains |
| Krovikan Horror | Thawing Glaciers | Plains |
| Krovikan Horror | Thawing Glaciers | Plains |
| **Pocket 2** | **Pocket 2** | **Pocket 2** |
| Knights of Stromgald | Enduring Renewal | Plains |
| Knights of Stromgald | Enduring Renewal | Plains |
| Knights of Stromgald | Enduring Renewal | Plains |
| Knights of Stromgald | Zuran Orb | Swamp |
| **Pocket 3** | **Pocket 3** | **Pocket 3** |
| Ashen Ghoul | Swords to Plowshares | Swamp |
| Ashen Ghoul | Swords to Plowshares | Swamp |
| Ashen Ghoul | Swords to Plowshares | Swamp |
| Ashen Ghoul | Swords to Plowshares | Swamp |
| **Pocket 4** | **Pocket 4** | **Pocket 4** |
| Wings of Aesthir | Disenchant | Swamp |
| Wings of Aesthir | Disenchant | Swamp |
| Wings of Aesthir | Disenchant | Swamp |
| Wings of Aesthir | Icequake | Swamp |
| **Pocket 5** | **Pocket 5** | **Pocket 5** |
| Shield Sphere | Icequake | Swamp |
| Shield Sphere | Plains | Swamp |
| Shield Sphere | Plains | Swamp |
| Shield Sphere | Plains | Swamp |

**Sideboard**

1. Icequake
2. Icequake
3. Disenchant
4. Exile
5. Exile
6. Exile
7. Kjeldoran Outpost
8. C.O.P. Green
9. C.O.P. Green
10. C.O.P. White
11. C.O.P. Red
12. C.O.P. Red
13. Loadstone Bauble
14. Loadstone Bauble
15. Loadstone Bauble

# The Hat Cap Deck

| Block 1 | Block 2 | Block 3 |
|---|---|---|
| **Pocket 1** | **Pocket 1** | **Pocket 1** |
| Jester's Cap | Binding Grasp | Adarkar Wastes |
| Jester's Cap | Binding Grasp | Adarkar Wastes |
| Jester's Cap | Binding Grasp | Adarkar Wastes |
| Jester's Cap | Power Sink | Adarkar Wastes |
| **Pocket 2** | **Pocket 2** | **Pocket 2** |
| Helm of Obedience | Blinking Spirit | Island |
| Helm of Obedience | Blinking Spirit | Island |
| Helm of Obedience | Blinking Spirit | Island |
| Power Sink | Power Sink | Island |
| **Pocket 3** | **Pocket 3** | **Pocket 3** |
| Swords to Plowshares | Stone Rain | Island |
| Swords to Plowshares | Stone Rain | Island |
| Swords to Plowshares | Kjeldoran Outpost | Island |
| Swords to Plowshares | Kjeldoran Outpost | Island |
| **Pocket 4** | **Pocket 4** | **Pocket 4** |
| Disenchant | Thawing Glaciers | Island |
| Disenchant | Thawing Glaciers | Plains |
| Disenchant | Thawing Glaciers | Plains |
| Zuran Orb | Force of Will | Plains |
| **Pocket 5** | **Pocket 5** | **Pocket 5** |
| Counterspell | Force of Will | Plains |
| Counterspell | Force of Will | Plains |
| Counterspell | Mountain | Plains |
| Counterspell | Mountain | Plains |

**Sideboard**

1. C.O.P. White
2. C.O.P. White
3. C.O.P. White
4. C.O.P. Green
5. C.O.P. Green
6. Mountain
7. Stone Rain
8. Loadstone Bauble
9. Loadstone Bauble
10. Loadstone Bauble
11. Exile
12. Exile
13. Exile
14. Disenchant
15. Binding Grasp

# The Browse Digger Deck

| Block 1 | Block 2 | Block 3 |
|---------|---------|---------|
| **Pocket 1** | **Pocket 1** | **Pocket 1** |
| Browse | Force of Will | Adarkar Wastes |
| Browse | Force of Will | Adarkar Wastes |
| Browse | Force of Will | Adarkar Wastes |
| Browse | Force of Will | Adarkar Wastes |
| **Pocket 2** | **Pocket 2** | **Pocket 2** |
| Soldevi Digger | Disenchant | Plains |
| Soldevi Digger | Disenchant | Plains |
| Kjeldoran Outpost | Disenchant | Plains |
| Kjeldoran Outpost | Zuran Orb | Plains |
| **Pocket 3** | **Pocket 3** | **Pocket 3** |
| Jester's Cap | Swords to Plowshares | Island |
| Jester's Cap | Swords to Plowshares | Island |
| Jester's Cap | Swords to Plowshares | Island |
| Jester's Cap | Swords to Plowshares | Island |
| **Pocket 4** | **Pocket 4** | **Pocket 4** |
| Counterspell | Binding Grasp | Plains |
| Counterspell | Binding Grasp | Plains |
| Counterspell | Binding Grasp | Plains |
| Counterspell | Thawing Glaciers | Plains |
| **Pocket 5** | **Pocket 5** | **Pocket 5** |
| Power Sink | Thawing Glaciers | Island |
| Power Sink | Thawing Glaciers | Island |
| Power Sink | Island | Island |
| Power Sink | Island | Island |

**Sideboard**

1. Mishra's Groundbreaker
2. Mishra's Groundbreaker
3. Mishra's Groundbreaker
4. Binding Grasp
5. Disenchant
6. Exile
7. Exile
8. Exile
9. Hydroblast
10. Hydroblast
11. Loadstone Bauble
12. Loadstone Bauble
13. Loadstone Bauble
14. C.O.P. White
15. C.O.P. White

**124**

# *The Alliances Necro Deck*

| Block 1 | Block 2 | Block 3 |
|---|---|---|
| **Pocket 1** | **Pocket 1** | **Pocket 1** |
| Soul Burn | Horror Shade | Underground River |
| Soul Burn | Horror Shade | Underground River |
| Soul Burn | Horror Shade | Underground River |
| Soul Burn | Despotic Scepter | Underground River |
| **Pocket 2** | **Pocket 2** | **Pocket 2** |
| Necropotence | Dark Ritual | Island |
| Necropotence | Dark Ritual | Island |
| Necropotence | Dark Ritual | Swamp |
| Zuran Orb | Dark Ritual | Swamp |
| **Pocket 3** | **Pocket 3** | **Pocket 3** |
| Knights of Stromgald | Lake of the Dead | Swamp |
| Knights of Stromgald | Soldevi Adnate | Swamp |
| Knights of Stromgald | Soldevi Adnate | Swamp |
| Knights of Stromgald | Soldevi Adnate | Swamp |
| **Pocket 4** | **Pocket 4** | **Pocket 4** |
| Lim-Dûl's High Guard | Feast or Famine | Swamp |
| Lim-Dûl's High Guard | Feast or Famine | Swamp |
| Lim-Dûl's High Guard | Feast or Famine | Swamp |
| Lim-Dûl's High Guard | Thawing Glaciers | Swamp |
| **Pocket 5** | **Pocket 5** | **Pocket 5** |
| Phantasmal Fiend | Thawing Glaciers | Swamp |
| Phantasmal Fiend | Thawing Glaciers | Swamp |
| Phantasmal Fiend | Swamp | Swamp |
| Phantasmal Fiend | Swamp | Swamp |

## Sideboard

1. Hydroblast
2. Hydroblast
3. Hydroblast
4. Hydroblast
5. Word of Undoing
6. Word of Undoing
7. Word of Undoing
8. Word of Undoing
9. Infernal Darkness
10. Infernal Darkness
11. Dark Banishing
12. Dark Banishing
13. Dark Banishing
14. Feast or Famine
15. Despotic Scepter

# *Index*

Also available from Wordware Publishing, Inc.

**Baxter on Magic: A Guide to Proper Playing Techniques for Magic: The Gathering™**
by George H. Baxter
180 pages • 6 x 9
ISBN: 1-55622-523-7 $12.95

**Mastering Magic™ Cards**
by Larry W. Smith, Ph.D.
and George H. Baxter
Foreword by Richard Garfield,
Creator of Magic Cards
240 pages • 6 x 9
ISBN: 1-55622-457-5 $15.95

**Deep Magic Advanced Strategies for Experienced Players of Magic: The Gathering™**
by Charles Wolfe and George H. Baxter
240 pages • 6 x 9
ISBN: 1-55622-461-3 $14.95

**Pro Magic: The Art of Professional Deck Construction**
by George H. Baxter
180 pages • 6 x 9
ISBN: 1-55622-524-5 $12.95

**Dominating Dominia™**
by George H. Baxter
208 pages • 6 x 9
ISBN: 1-55622-491-5 $12.95

**Single Card Strategies for Magic: The Gathering™**
by Jeff S. Franzmann, Philip Kramer, and Beth Moursund
200 pages • 6 x 9
ISBN: 1-55622-489-3 $14.95

**Learn Magic™ Cards**
by Larry W. Smith, Ph.D.
144 pages • 6 x 9
ISBN: 1-55622-460-5 $9.95

**The Tables of Magic**
by George H. Baxter
160 pages • 6 x 9
ISBN: 1-55622-486-9 $9.95

**Magic Cards Simplified For Player Parents and Beginners of Magic: The Gathering™**
by George H. Baxter and Russell A. Stultz
112 pages • 6 x 9
ISBN: 1-55622-522-9 $7.95

For more information or to order, contact:

**Wordware Publishing, Inc.**
1506 Capital Avenue
Plano, Texas 75074
(214) 423-0090